D1289974

*Praise for*
# One Friday in Jerusalem

*One Friday in Jerusalem* is the most refreshing glimpse I have ever had into a Palestinian Maronite Christian's deep personal experiences and spiritual insights. Having lived in Jerusalem, I appreciate Andre's accurate and vivid descriptions of the Via Dolorosa, and I was riveted to the book as I walked each step, gleaning valuable insights. Andre neither defends nor undermines the traditional stations of the cross; rather, he shares an insider's spiritual pilgrimage. His knowledge of history and its importance in understanding Jerusalem's modern conflicts makes this book a must-read.

—DONALD L. BRAKE SR., PhD, Dean Emeritus, Multnomah Biblical Seminary, and Author of *Jesus, A Visual History: The Dramatic Story of the Messiah in the Holy Land*

After ten trips to Israel, I've tried many tour guides; Andre is the best, both in teaching and in professional guiding services. As a pastor who specializes in teaching the Bible, I consider Andre *my* pastor, guide, and instant-answer-man for helping me understand Israel. I am so glad he has put his experience with the Lord in writing. I trust that this book will help many who have walked the Via Dolorosa continue their own journey to the cross with Christ. And if you have never been to Israel, please make this journey to the Holy Land a priority in life.

—主仆 谢 庆 福 牧 师  REV. SAMUEL SIA,
St. Stephen's Parish, Manila, The Philippines

I have known Andre for many years. He has made a tremendous impact on our church. His story of growing up on the streets of Jerusalem is powerful, life changing, and one you won't want to miss.

—BRANDON BEALS, Pastor, Canyon Creek Church, Seattle, Washington


This is a powerful literary work that reveals the times, the country, and the people of the Holy Land, both historically and today. Andre lends personal insights and a wealth of knowledge and revelation about Israel and about Christ. *One Friday in Jerusalem* takes you to the ancient streets those of us in Andre's tour groups have walked as, led by him, we have encountered the reality and magnitude of the Via Dolarosa.

—BISHOP RAYMOND W JOHNSON, Living Faith Christian Center, Baton Rouge, Louisiana

# ONE FRIDAY in JERUSALEM

## WALKING TO CALVARY—a Tour, a Faith, a Life

# ANDRE MOUBARAK

*To my beloved wife, Marie—*
*my best friend, comforter, counselor, and*
*partner in ministry and life . . .*
*To my dad, whose love and example*
*have meant the world to me,*
*and whom I deeply miss . . .*
*To my mom, whose heart and care*
*for me have seen me through*
*the best and worst in life . . .*
*Thank you!*

# Contents

## PART 3: Beyond the Tomb

# Foreword

If you visit the Holy Land more than once, you will discover for yourself that the Holy Spirit provides you with new insights on every journey you make. I recently returned from my fourth trip to Israel. One of the insights I brought home with me from my last trip was the sad reality that people can live just a few hundred feet from where Jesus was born, lived, ministered, died, and was raised from the dead and still never have one meaningful encounter with the living Christ. Perhaps it would be like living near the Lincoln Memorial, knowing that there was once a man named Abraham Lincoln but never really encountering him as anything more than an important figure in history.

Andre's book is the story of a Palestinian man who doesn't just know the Jesus of history but who is met by the living Christ who encounters people's hearts today. Andre doesn't just know the land of Jesus; he knows the Jesus of the land. This is the story of a little boy whose playground was the backdrop of the ages, but then whose heart became the home of the One who forever split the timeline and rent the veil between heaven and earth.

I first met Andre on my second trip to Israel. I sensed a divine connection with him the very moment I met him and was immediately impressed with how hungry he was for the Holy Spirit. Our meeting resulted in my visiting what was at that time the only charismatic fellowship of Palestinian believers in the city of Jerusalem. They represented the most marginalized and persecuted group of people in all of Israel: rejected by many Israelis for being Palestinian; rejected by many Jews and Muslims for being Christians; rejected by many Christians for believing that the gifts of the Holy Spirit and supernatural encounters with God are for today. Yet instead of meeting a group of offended, cynical, dualistic, and defensive people, I met some the most hospitable, forgiving, and loving people on the planet.

How does this happen? The answers lie within the pages of this book. It's a story of forgiveness, redemption, and the power of the Holy Spirit to take someone whose heart had been wounded in one of the most complicated racial, political, and religious climates of the world and turn him into a lover of Jesus and a lover of people regardless of their race, political views, or religion.

Andre carries a gift to help people encounter the real Jesus—the Jesus who teaches us to love people who hate us, to pray for people who hurt us, to bless people who curse us, to give a second mile to those who have already taken one mile from us. Don't just read this book—let it read you. Through it, let the Holy Spirit help you know the real Jesus, and as you do, let the real Jesus answer the question "Who is my neighbor?"

NATHANAEL WOLF
Pastor, Gateway Centre Church

# Acknowledgments

This journey would not have been possible without the support of my family, mentors, and friends. To my family: Thank you for encouraging me in all of my pursuits and inspiring me to follow my dreams.

I am especially grateful to my wife, Marie Howanstine Moubarak, who supported me emotionally. I always knew you believed in me and wanted the best for me. Thank you for teaching me that my job in life is to learn, to be dedicated, and to work hard to be real and to know and understand others—for only then could I know and understand myself.

To my friends scattered around the country and the world: Thank you for your thoughts, prayers, phone calls, emails, texts, visits, and editing advice, and for being there whenever I needed a friend. You have enriched my life, and I look forward to continuing our relationships.

With deepest love and gratitude, thank you to my father, Mr. Joseph Antone Moubarak, to whom I owe more than I can say. I wish he were alive today. Thank you, Dad, for raising me as a man of God.

To my twin brother, Tony Moubarak: Thank you for your support. Thanks as well to my brothers Alfred and Albert Moubarak for standing with me in life and business, and to my mother, Reema Bajes Shaheen, for her love and care from my childhood on.

To John and Catherine Howanstine, my special father- and mother-in-law: For your continuous encouragement as I wrote this book—thank you.

Thank you, Shafiqa Hashweh, for your spiritual guidance, and Heather Luke, for your help in developing the story.

To Virginia Myers and Greg Baker: Thank you for your editorial help in smoothing out so many of the rough edges in the initial stages of my manuscript.

To Bishop Raymond W. Johnson of Living Faith Christian Center in Baton Rouge, Louisiana, USA: Thank you for being a constant source of support and encouragement, and a spiritual father and mentor. And thank you for your church's continuing partnership and prayers.

Finally, thank you to my professional team who helped me bring this book from a rough manuscript to a published reality: Beth Shagene, for her expertise and excellence in designing the interior; Vanessa Carroll, whose meticulous proofreading ensured a clean manuscript; Jeff Gifford, who created such a wonderful jacket; and my editor, Bob Hartig, who read my heart so clearly and, with patience and discernment, helped me translate it into print.

I am sure this book would never have been completed without all of you. I thank you all.

# Introduction

The Via Dolorosa—Latin for "Way of Grief," "Way of Sorrows," or "Painful Way"—is a street in the Old City of Jerusalem, held to be the route that Jesus walked on the way to his crucifixion. It is a distance of about six hundred meters (two thousand feet) but a one-hour walk with prayers and devotions.

I know the Via Dolorosa because I grew up on the Via Dolorosa. As a boy, I played on its winding pathway, and for many years I have guided pilgrims retracing the footsteps of Jesus from Pilate's praetorium to Calvary. I know every doorway, every window overhead, every arch and column, the color, texture, and peculiarities of its walls. If every stone in the pavement had a name, I could call out each one individually. The interiors of sites such as the Church of the Holy Sepulcher are as familiar to me as your living room is to you.

But this book is so much more than a guided tour of the Via Dolorosa. It is certainly that—it will steer you from one site to the next down the narrow, stony pathway. But it is also a guide to greater depth in your relationship with Jesus, to the wonders of God's Word, to lives lived in the shadow of persecution and the power of the cross, and to your own life. In taking you faithfully through the stations of the cross, it will also transport you far beyond them on an eye-opening journey through the Bible, set against the background of Middle Eastern culture, customs, and history.

Very importantly, I hope this book will help you personalize, to the extent such a thing is possible, what Jesus endured as He bore His cross along the "Way of Sorrow." I want these pages to awaken your imagination, your emotions, and your heart so you will feel something of what Jesus might have felt and seen and thought, and so appreciate all the more the price He paid for you and me on that tragic, glorious day of His crucifixion. I hope this will be your experience as you read.

By the request of the many groups I have guided, this book will also share my personal story as a Palestinian Maronite Arab Christian. (For a detailed discussion of the Maronites, see appendix A.) Growing up here in the roily tension zone of three great world religions—Christianity, Judaism, and Islam—I connect intimately with each one of the stations of the cross. As I share with you key passages of my life, I hope you will see in some of them reflections of your own life—for we all, each one of us, are bearing crosses of different sizes, shapes, and weights down our own Via Dolorosas. And the Spirit of Jesus is carrying us along beyond our griefs toward a glory greater than we can imagine.

Finally, I hope this book will awaken you to the plight of your brothers and sisters here in Jerusalem and in the Middle East. I desire that you will feel moved . . .

*by compassion*, as you hear the stories of these dark streets and darker lives;

*by wonder*, as you learn how God is actively changing men and women—Jews, Muslims, and Christians alike—in miraculous ways through the light of the gospel, the love of Jesus, and the power of the Holy Spirit;

*to action*, as you discover how *you* can come alongside your brothers and sisters here in the Middle East—and why it is so important, for both our sake and your own, that you do so.

## How This Book Is Organized

I, Andre Yousef Antone Moubarak, am a Palestinian Maronite Arab Christian from the lesser known Christian Quarter of the Old City of Jerusalem. I am one of the "living stones" who make up the church of Jesus here in Jerusalem.[1] I did not choose to become a tour guide. My profession chose me and became a way of life, my vocation and destiny. I have guided countless people from all over the world—from the United States, China, Singapore, South Africa, Philippines, the United Kingdom, Australia, Germany, Sweden, Mexico, Argentina, Brazil, Africa, Iceland, and others I can no longer recall. Almost every group advised me to write down the valuable information I shared with them.

Then on September 11, 2009, while praying in my Jerusalem apartment, I felt the Holy Spirit enfolding me with His peace and love, and the thought impressed itself in my mind: *the stations of the cross.* That thought has developed into this book.

The first fourteen chapters, divided evenly into parts 1 and 2, correspond to the fourteen stations of the cross and also to fourteen stations of my personal life—for I, as a Palestinian Christian, have carried my own cross as part of a despised minority in the Holy Land and the Middle East.

In part 3, the final two chapters celebrate the resurrection and the life-changing power of Jesus. As dark and depressing as the neighborhood of the present-day Via Dolorosa is, there is hope for the people who live there—and hope for your own life, wherever you live and whatever you may be facing. You will read stories of how this hope has become real in the lives of men and women who have encountered the transforming reality of the risen, victorious Jesus.

## *The Three Icons*

Because this book seeks to accomplish several purposes, it uses three different icons to highlight significant sections. The icons will help you orient yourself visually to changes in the topic and tone.

The **"Taking the Tour"** icon indicates the tour-guide aspect of the text. Its content is, for the most part, practical and matter-of-fact, directing you from one station to the next and describing points of interest. Explicit directions are boldfaced for your convenience.

**"Insights for Your Heart"** is usually quite different in tone from "Taking the Tour." My goal here is to share insights and inspiration from Scripture from a Middle Eastern point of view in a way that speaks to your imagination and emotions, so that the biblical account comes alive for you in the context of your own life.

**"Tales from My Life"** is exactly what it says. I share different, deeply personal aspects of my life as a Palestinian Christian and connect them with the different stations of the cross.

Each chapter opens with an introduction to set the tone, then proceeds to "Taking the Tour." From there, the order and number of the icons differ from chapter to chapter, and the length of sections can sometimes vary greatly from one to the next. Moreover, there is not always a hard line between the content of the icons. View the icons as road signs, not inflexible boundaries. You may come across an insight that speaks to your heart in one of my life stories, or you may find a spiritual truth in "Taking the Tour" that you might expect to find in "Insights for Your Heart." The book is organic; the icons simply clue you in to a section's overall focus.

## Middle Eastern Insights

Jesus was a Jew. Oddly, this basic truth was a profound revelation for me as a Palestinian boy, and it can be just as illuminating for Western Christians who, though acknowledging Jesus's ethnicity in their minds, have never really grasped its implications.

Jesus was born as a Jew in Bethlehem. He spent his boyhood learning the Torah like any other religious Jewish child in Nazareth. His ministry was that of a rabbi in Galilee. He was sacrificed as the Lamb of God during Passover in Jerusalem. And He will come back as a Jew, the Lion of Judah.

The Holy Land is where Jesus lived and where the events of the Old and New Testaments took place. This is why the Via Dolorosa, the Old City of Jerusalem, and this land in which I live are so important to me. Together they have shaped my heart, my identity, and my faith. We in the Middle East are intrinsically connected to this land and place of our birth—they are significant to our well-being. This is different from the thinking in most Western cultures, where people travel and migrate from one country to another. The land of their birth has less value to them.

Most modern Bible translations come from a Western mentality heavily influenced by the Greco-Roman theology that has pervaded the church since the early centuries. One of my objectives in this book is to explain the Bible's stories from a Middle Eastern perspective, framed by the way of life as it was. Once the Bible's culture, context, and customs are viewed from the Hebraic tradition rather than Western interpretations, the Scriptures come alive. As a tour guide, I strive to reawaken the first-century way of thinking—to return to the origins and beginnings of the early church.

Looking at Scripture from a Middle Eastern point of view brings three benefits:

1. What you already know is *confirmed*, and more details are added.

2. It is also *clarified* and expanded as you gain new information and insights. You'll deepen your knowledge and gain greater clarity for your life.

3. Misconceptions are *corrected*. The Hebraic perspective will help you accurately grasp the Scriptures where your understanding may be biased or incomplete.

Where was Jesus born? What was the place like where He grew up and played? Where did He die? Let's adjust our spiritual eyes and ears to first-century sight and hearing. Then, should you visit this land in person—and I so hope you will—you'll build an even deeper understanding based on the new viewpoint and knowledge you've acquired. This theme drives every tour and is the foundation stone of my teachings. The result is always greater confidence in Jesus's dominion and divinity.

■ ■ ■

One last thing: Part of my vision for this book is to bring kingdom transformation to the depression and sadness of the streets of the Christian Quarter. I long to see God's people begin to shine here in the darkness and for a royal army to spread the King's glory all over Israel. We Palestinian Christians are a treasure buried in the heart of Jerusalem, covered by rocks of offense, thorns of treachery, and relics of religion. But great things can happen when you pray for us and reach out to us. I hope this book will inspire you—your ministry, your church, your group, or simply you yourself—to come to this land of the Bible and meet with us, your brothers and sisters in Jesus Christ, the "living stones" of Jerusalem.

# Prologue

The voice came suddenly, no more than an urgent whisper.

"Andre, move. *Right now!*"

For a moment I thought my friend who was with me had spoken to me. But he hadn't, nor had anyone else out on bustling Ben Yehuda Street in West Jerusalem.

It was December 1, 2001, and a beautiful evening for wandering the central city. The time was shortly before midnight, but Kikar Tzion, Zion Square, is always busy, especially on a Saturday night, when it is full of young people hanging out after the Sabbath ends. Countless times I had been among them, enjoying the fun and excitement. Yet tonight I felt inexplicably tense. Something was wrong—I knew it in my gut.

Was I just being hypersensitive? Maybe. But the feeling wouldn't go away. In fact, it was getting stronger. . . .

"Andre, MOVE! NOW!"

The voice was louder—but whose was it? People were everywhere, but other than my friend, there was no one I knew. Was I hearing things?

*Must be my imagination. Just ignore it.*

Seconds later, I felt someone pushing me, shoving me across

Zion Square toward Jaffa Street. But it wasn't my friend—he was following several paces behind. No one was near me. Yet something that felt like a gust of wind was holding my arms, legs, and body and propelling me forward.

Now I really was freaked out. *I must be drunk*—but I hadn't had even a sip of beer.

The Café Aroma on Jaffa Street was just ahead of me. Shaken, I went inside and sat down.

BOOM!

The windows shattered and my body felt the jolt of a tremendous explosion. I could see debris flying and blood splattering, hear people screaming in pain and horror. And immediately I knew. Bomb attack!

My first impulse was to make sure I was still in one piece. My second was to pray. Half consciously, I made a vow: "Lord, if I live, I will give you my life."

My life? Like a fast-motion movie, it flashed across my mind. What had I achieved with it? The answer hit me hard: nothing. Although I was a believer, saved by the blood of Jesus Christ, I did not take my faith seriously. Growing up, I just went with the flow, my faith sometimes up and sometimes down.

But just now I had been only feet from death. The shock of the bomb and my proximity to it seemed unreal, impossible to grasp. Yet suddenly I realized how precious my faith truly was.

Just as swiftly, my natural fears gripped me. I was a Palestinian. The Jews would take revenge on me if they caught me here. I had to get home.

Outside the coffee shop was a nightmare of blood and glass. All the windows in the area had been blown out by the force of the explosion. Hundreds of screaming young adults were running from the blast site. But I had heard that in the event of a bombing, the best response is to stay still, not run. So I resisted the urge to flee.

BOOOOM! A second powerful explosion, even louder than the first, rocked the street. And now the same panicked crowd was stampeding back my way. I froze. What should I do? If they noticed me, they'd assume I was part of the attack, and my life would not last a moment longer than it took them to lay their hands on me.

A backstreet branched off Jaffa Road and went through the Russian Compound. I hastened down it toward New Gate, the nearest entrance to the Christian Quarter, where I lived with my parents and brothers. While I was en route, a third bomb exploded, less powerful than the first two but still lethal. The beautiful night had become a nightmare.

Once through the New Gate, I passed my old high school and hurried down the steps by St. Saviour's church and down Christian Quarter Road to my house. I had completely forgotten about my friend, though I learned later he had made it out and was safe.

The time was half past midnight when I slipped inside and turned on the television. The news was all about the Hamas bomb attacks, the first two of which had been suicide bombers and the last a car bomb. I feared I might be on TV, but I had left before the journalists and cameras could arrive. It was too early for casualties to be announced; I watched for fifteen minutes and then went to bed.

But I was too terrified to sleep. I had almost lost my life.

■　■　■

Jerusalem, turbulent City of Peace. For thousands of Christians on pilgrimage every year, it is their destination; for me, it is my home. Here in the Christian Quarter of the Old City I was born and raised. The religious and historical sites that people from all around the world come to see, the ancient pavements that believers of every nation and culture travel thousands of miles to walk—these are my neighborhood. I know them like I know myself; indeed, they are a part of who I am. Jerusalem's stories are a part of my story, and my story is a tiny fragment of Jerusalem's.

The account I shared with you, terrifying as it was, does not define Jerusalem. There is much more to this city I love than violence and religious and ethnic tension. This is a vibrant place, a cosmopolitan town where nationalities and cultures flow together in colors as rich and varied as the clothes you see people wearing in its streets, as exotic as the many different languages you hear, and as fascinating as the mannerisms and traditions in constant enactment all around you. It is a city where people pursue their dreams, fall in love, raise their families, earn their livings, and long for the best in life for themselves and their children, just as you do. All of these things are a part of the story of Jerusalem. There is darkness, but there is also beauty, and light, and creativity, and industriousness, and promise.

Above all, there is hope—great hope. Hope for the people in my community. Hope for this city. And hope for you and your own life, wherever you live. For among the many stories of Jerusalem—those of centuries past and those yet to be written—one story stands above all others. It is the greatest story of all: the story of Jesus, the Son of God, who gave His life that you and I might have life. His power to change hearts and lives is real. I have seen it in my own life and in the lives of others. I have seen natural enemies brought together in their hearts by the Holy Spirit. I have witnessed desperate men and women transformed by the discovery of how much God loves them.

Only Jesus can do that. There is no other hope. But the hope and the love Jesus offers are powerful beyond anything we can grasp.

■  ■  ■

On a stretch of narrow street only two thousand feet long in Old Jerusalem, the story of redemptive history drew to its agonizing, glorious climax. Today countless believers visit the Via Dolorosa, intent on tracing the footsteps of Jesus. Whether they tread the exact physical path He followed on His way to His crucifixion is beside the point; the real value of the pilgrimage lies in the journey of the heart a person takes from one station of the cross to the next. For it is in the heart that Christ lives and dwells; the stones of the Via Dolorosa are simply points of contact that bring to life the cost of salvation for Christians of many stripes. Catholic, Orthodox, and Protestant alike come from all over the world to contemplate the passion of Jesus Christ in the place where it happened.

The place where I grew up.

The winding Via Dolorosa was my playground as a boy. It was there that I played soccer and hide-and-seek with my friends. The eighth station of the cross was my backyard, so to speak. The storied stones, walls, and pillars have been part of my everyday life from my earliest memories.

But the physical street is just a reflection of a deeper, spiritual Via Dolorosa. That Via Dolorosa is one which, in ways unique to each of us, we all must travel as followers of Jesus. He experienced the Way of Sorrow deeply, and so must we. Each station of the cross possesses a personal meaning for you and me; each is a mirror of how we come to know "the fellowship of [Christ's] sufferings" in our own life (Phil. 3:10).

This has surely been the case for me. And so, as in this book I guide you through the Old City down the Via Dolorosa—as I walk you through the fourteen stations of the cross, showing you centuries-old religious sites and describing their remarkable histories—I will also tell you my own story as well as that of Jesus, who is the reason this short, cramped street has such profound significance. I will share with you not only what I know as a professional tour guide but also what I have learned as a disciple. My desire is to help you identify with Jesus as you journey down your own Via Dolorosa, whatever it may look like—and beyond it to the matchless power and life-giving hope of the resurrection.

I also hope to stir your heart for Christians who live under

persecution—for us, your Jewish, Palestinian, and Arab brothers and sisters in Christ who, in dark corners of the Middle East,
remain faithful to our Messiah and yours.

As your guide, I promise you a colorful experience full of
insights that will engage your senses, your imagination, and most
importantly, your heart. Not all of it will be pleasant, for the Via
Dolorosa is a dark and dirty street. But that is how the way of the
cross was for Jesus, who transformed it into a pathway to light
and life.

Are you ready to take the journey? Then let us begin.

# PART 1

# Stations One through Seven

# CHAPTER 1

# Jesus Is Condemned
# to Death

Walking the Via Dolorosa inside the ancient, walled Old City is an experience to treasure. I like it best on Fridays amid the jostling crowds. You pass Palestinian merchants selling their wares. You weave among Christian monks from different denominations hastening to the 3:00 p.m. devotional walk. Imams crisscross your path, heading for prayer at the Al-Aqsa Mosque on the Temple Mount, and Jewish rabbis brush by on their way to the Western Wall to pray before the Sabbath begins. Tourists from all over the world mill about, eager to walk the way of the cross. And all the while, edgy Israeli soldiers are checking local people's identity cards.

STATION I

The sights, set in modern Jerusalem, evoke the atmosphere and drama of these same streets two thousand years ago. But the events that led to the stations of the cross did not start here. They began hours earlier in a much more intimate setting as Jesus took bread and wine with His disciples, and as he solemnly proclaimed, "He who dipped his hand with me in the dish will betray me" (Matt. 26:23). And they continued with a trip to a local garden.

# ♡ It Began in a Garden

Leaving the upper room where he had shared the Passover meal
with those closest to him, Jesus "went out with His disciples over
the Brook Kidron, where there was a garden, which He and His
disciples entered" (John 18:1). The garden was Gethsemane on the
Mount of Olives.

But why there? Why a garden?

The tomb where Jesus's body was laid was also in a garden.
Obviously gardens are very important in this drama. Millen-
nia before, at the dawn of history—long before Moses led Israel
between the water walls of the Red Sea to deliverance on its far
shore; before Jacob wrestled with God in the darkness on the back-
side of the desert; before Adonai called Abraham forth from his
tent to behold a night sky glistening with promise—Adam walked
with God in a garden.

> The LORD God took the man and put him in the garden of
> Eden to tend and keep it.                              (GEN. 2:15)

But the devil came to Adam and Eve in the form of a creature
in that garden, leading to their separation from God. The intimacy
humans had enjoyed with God, and God with them, was broken.

It took another Adam, Jesus Christ (1 Cor. 15:45), to enter
another garden in order to create a new humanity—a new Adam
and a new Eve walking once again in communion with their
Creator.

And a new garden:

> [The angel] showed me a pure river of water of life, clear as
> crystal, proceeding from the throne of God and of the Lamb.
> In the middle of its street, and on either side of the river, was
> the tree of life, which bore twelve fruits, each tree yielding its
> fruit every month. The leaves of the tree were for the healing of

the nations. And there shall be no more curse, but the throne of God and of the Lamb shall be in it, and His servants shall serve Him.                                    (REV. 22: 1–3)

In Gethsemane the devil tempted Jesus just as he tempted Eve, and through Eve, Adam. This time, Satan came not as a serpent but as a familiar friend, Judas Iscariot. But Jesus, unlike the first Adam, resisted the temptation, giving his own life in order to vanquish death. Countering Adam's treason in Eden, with its tragic consequences, Jesus's faithfulness in Gethsemane unlocked the garden gate to the tree of life. I think His deepest, most intense pain began well before the first spike pierced his wrist on Golgotha. It started in Gethsemane.

That name, Gethsemane, has the same meaning in both Aramaic and Hebrew. *Gat* means "press" and *shemen* means "oil," and Gethsemane therefore means "oil press." In Gethsemane, the fruit of the trees that grew on the Mount of Olives was crushed to release its precious oil. You can see this same process still in operation today at ancient olive oil presses in the Holy Land.

The more an olive is crushed, the more oil it gives. That is what happened with Jesus in Gethsemane: like an olive, He was pressed relentlessly. That is also how it is with you and me. The more crushing we endure in our life and ministry, the more anointed we will become.

The most resilient part of an olive is its pit. It is hard to crush. But when it is crushed, it imparts a bitter kick that is the hallmark of a top-grade olive oil. Too much bitterness will ruin the oil, but the right amount is highly desirable, making for the very best flavor.

Do not run away when you are crushed. God knows what kind of pressure and how much is right for you. Commit yourself to Him and wait. Wait just a little longer. Crushing is the divine process that can, if you will let it, allow the Holy Spirit to instill His presence powerfully in your life and release you to your destiny.

■ ■ ■

We know what followed in Gethsemane: Men's voices and the tramp of feet disrupting the silence. Soldiers confronting the little band of disciples, and at their forefront, a familiar face, the face of Judas. A kiss of betrayal, rough hands laid on Jesus, panic-stricken desertion by His closest friends, and then, under guard, a hard walk out of the garden to physical brutalization and a mockery of a trial.

Thus Jesus started his journey down the Via Dolorosa itself. Let us begin tracing his footsteps.

## ✖ The First Station

The first station of the Via Dolorosa, commemorating Jesus's sentencing to death by Pontius Pilate, is at the site of today's Madrasa Al-Omariyeh elementary school for local Muslim boys. The *madrasa* (Arabic for "school") is located 1,300 meters (four fifths of a mile) northwest of the Lion's Gate at the northwest corner of the ancient Temple Mount, on top of the remains of the Antonia Fortress. It is across the street from the Franciscan Convent of the Flagellation.

Let me guide you there from outside Herod's Gate on the eastern side of the Old City. Most of my groups arrive by bus from the hotel, and we walk from the bus stop to our destination through the heart of the Muslim Quarter.

Outside the Old City you see mostly older men and women, but once inside Herod's Gate you'll see many boys and girls—alone, in pairs, and in small groups. No adults hover over them; the children's safety is taken for granted. Approaching the first station of the cross, you can hear their voices down the street, mingled with those of their teachers. When I am guiding groups, I start the Via Dolorosa early in the morning; otherwise the crowds of children heading to their classes can make the tour more like a complicated dance than a walk!

The main entrance to the Al-Omariyeh school is a gray gate, and if you look toward the steps on the right, just before the gate you will see a round plaque with the Roman numeral I.

Al-Omariyeh is a private Muslim school and is not set up as an official tourist site. It can only be entered with the caretaker's permission, and then only at certain times in the afternoon after school is finished.

Once inside, head to the right and you'll reach the school's courtyard—a large, open plaza, said to be the site of the Antonia Fortress, named by King Herod in honor of Mark Antony. The Antonia was both a Roman military headquarters and a barracks for the soldiers. The first-century Jewish historian Josephus Flavius repeatedly refers to it as "the tower Antonia" and says it was built by the Jewish high priest Johanan Hyrcanus, who ruled from (142–63 BC) under the Hasmonean dynasty. Originally intended for the safekeeping of the holy vestments worn on Passover, Yom Kippur, and other important Jewish religious days, it was far smaller than is often supposed.

The tower gave the Roman soldiers and governor a panoramic view of the temple complex. This was especially useful for preventing uprisings during Jewish festivals, when Jewish crowds outnumbered the Roman soldiers. Keeping the *Pax Romana*, the Peace of the Roman Empire, was of utmost importance.

The Antonia Fortress was the seat of Pontius Pilate and may have been the place of the hall of judgment. However, some scholars believe the Roman governor's hall of judgment, or praetorium, was never located in the Antonia but that the drama with Pilate unfolded inside King Herod's grand palace at the western corner of the Old City near Jaffa Gate. The Bible says simply that the Jewish leaders "led Jesus from Caiaphas to the Praetorium" (John 18:28), where Pilate "delivered Him to them to be crucified" (John 19:16). (For more on the praetorium, see appendix D.)

Both Herod's palace and the Antonia Fortress were destroyed by the army of Titus during the siege of Jerusalem in AD 70. Today in the area of the Antonia site on the Via Dolorosa, you will see the stone archway and gray dome of the Church of Ecce Homo, now a part of the Notre Dame de Sion Convent.

## ♡ Pilate: Guilt That Won't Wash

> Pilate, when he had called together the chief priests, the rulers, and the people, said to them, "You have brought this Man to me, as one who misleads the people. And indeed, having examined Him in your presence, I have found no fault in this Man concerning those things of which you accuse Him." . . .

But they were insistent, demanding with loud voices that He be crucified. And the voices of these men and of the chief priests prevailed. So Pilate gave sentence that it should be as they requested. . . . He delivered Jesus to their will.

(LUKE 23:13–14, 23–25)

Was Pilate just a helpless tool caught in the pincers of Roman and Jewish politics? Some Christian commentators have tried to exonerate him as a truth-seeking man who caved to intense pressure from the Sanhedrin (the Jewish court) and the demands of an unruly crowd. Left to himself, he never would have crucified Jesus.

But this overlooks Pilate's cruelty. He frequently offended and grossly mistreated the Jewish people. The Jewish historian Josephus records an instance when Pilate took money given to the Jerusalem temple and used it for one of his own projects. Then when a crowd of Jews objected, Pilate killed many of them.[2] Luke's gospel records a similar instance when Pilate mingled the blood of some Galilean Jews with their temple sacrifices (Luke 13:1). And first-century Jewish philosopher Philo of Alexandria accused Pilate of "briberies, insults, robberies, outrages, wanton injustices, constantly repeated executions without trial, and ceaseless and grievous cruelty."[3]

It is unlikely that Pilate would have been forced by Jewish leaders and the crowd to act against his will. As a well-informed governor, he was surely aware of Jesus's widespread popularity with ordinary Jewish people. This would have concerned him, especially during the Passover, when Jerusalem's normal population of around thirty-five thousand swelled to perhaps ten times that number. But ordering Jesus's execution under Roman law might have led to revolt. So while it is likely that Pilate wanted Jesus to die, he wanted Him to be sentenced under Jewish religious law.

Pilate needed a way to use his authority to put Jesus to death while publicly washing his hands of the decision—and he found that way. Cleverly playing with the Jewish leaders and their sup-porters, he rid himself of Jesus while deflecting any popular anger toward the leaders and away from himself and Rome.

Roman governors rarely lasted long at their posts, particularly if they were unsuccessful at keeping the peace. Jesus was a threat to Roman order because for three years He had proclaimed the kingdom of God, not the rule of Caesar, and in His answers to Pilate, He never rejected the charge that He claimed to be King of the Jews.

It is important to establish Pilate's guilt in the death of Jesus as a counterargument to the historical anti-Semitic tendency among some Christians (including, for many centuries the Roman Catho-lic Church) to blame "the Jews" for the death of Jesus.

##  A Shocking Revelation

In the Catholic school of my boyhood, I was taught that the Jews were my enemies and that they had crucified my Jesus. They never told us that Jesus Himself was Jewish. I thought Jesus was Catholic and spoke only Aramaic! Only later did I learn that, although most of the Jewish *leaders* in Jerusalem wanted Jesus killed (multitudes of the Jewish common people loved Him), Pilate also had a central role in Jesus's death.

One day as I was walking to school, a friend mentioned that Jesus was Jewish. *What!* I demanded that he say it again. He repeated confidently that Jesus was Jewish.

I almost hit my friend. Surely he had blasphemed! The Jews had crucified Jesus, so there could be no way that Jesus Himself was a Jew. Besides, Jews in general were the enemies of us Palestinians, so how could the Jesus I loved have been Jewish?

Confused, I spent the next week repeatedly asking my teacher, my father, and others the same question: Was Jesus Jewish? Was He? *Was Jesus Jewish?*

They all answered yes.

So it was that, at age eight, I received my first revelation about Jesus's identity—and it changed my understanding of my own identity.

■ ■ ■

Jerusalem is a complex city whose political identity has changed many times over the centuries, depending on which nation most recently conquered it. Fascinating though Jerusalem is, so rich in its history and diversity, many people do not find it an easy place to live. My ethnicity and faith make me one of them.

I am a Palestinian Arab Christian born in Jerusalem in 1975. My mother's family is from Ein Areek, a Palestinian farming village near Ramallah. My father's family came from Jaffa. Both families fled their homes during the *Nakba*—the catastrophic Arab exodus that created the Palestinian refugee crisis in 1948, when the Jews won their War of Independence against the armies of the surrounding Arab states.

Through a series of decisions necessary for survival, both of my parents were living in the Old City of Jerusalem in 1967 when Israel captured it from the Jordanians. Suddenly my mom and dad found themselves living in Israel. Here in Jerusalem they met, married, and raised my twin brother and me. But the Israeli government never granted my family either citizenship or passports. Instead, like thousands of other Arabs in Jerusalem, we were issued blue residency cards that gave us no rights at all.

Although Israel offered local Arabs citizenship after it annexed East Jerusalem in 1967, most declined, hoping and believing that East Jerusalem would eventually become the capital of a Palestinian state. Accepting Israeli citizenship was seen as accepting Israeli sovereignty over Jerusalem. As for the rest with blue IDs, leaving the country, even for a year to study abroad, requires a special United Nations travel document for stateless people, called a laissez-passer visa. Travelers risk losing their ID and status if they stay away too long, meaning they can't return to their homes in Jerusalem.

My blue ID card condemned me to be a mistrusted, second-class Arab Christian—or worse. Israeli Jews often suspected me of being a terrorist because I am a Palestinian, while the Muslims saw me as a Zionist because I am a Christian who believes in the promises of the Bible, both the Old and New Testaments. Even after I received an Israeli passport, the general attitude and suspicion toward me by both Israelis and Arabs has remained the same. But I am not alone. This double-edged mistrust is part of the cost of being a Palestinian disciple of Jesus.

We Palestinian Christians are unknown to Christians elsewhere in the world, almost erased from the collective knowledge of humanity. I ask every group I guide if they know about Palestinian Christians. None of them realizes our community exists.

"When did you convert from being a Muslim to a Christian?" they want to know. I explain that neither I nor my ancestors have ever been Muslims. Our Christian faith harkens back to the early church, long before the West was Christianized. Yet even my future wife, an American, knew nothing of us when she first visited Jerusalem.

My background as a Palestinian Maronite Christian who grew up on the Via Dolorosa has necessarily connected me intimately with its story. As we tour this stony street, I hope to share that story with you, at various times, from three perspectives. They are a Jewish perspective, for Jesus was a Jew; a Christian perspective, given the influence of Catholicism and other Christian faiths; and a Muslim perspective, as the region was controlled by Muslims for the last nearly 1,300 years.

My personal story, parts of which are deeply painful and other parts glorious, is also part of *the* story—the story of the Via

Dolorosa two centuries ago and today. In the telling, I hope you will discover ways in which your own life also follows from one station of the cross to the next.

————

*Yes, Jesus, I can see Your pain in being treated like a traitor, like a criminal, when all You did was preach and practice love and God's forgiveness. Carry me with You up this path to Calvary, Lord, so that I too may learn how to be meek in even the most difficult situations of my life.*

# CHAPTER 2

# Jesus Takes Up
# the Cross

The Old City of Jerusalem is a mosaic of ancient churches dating back to New Testament times on up through the centuries. The earliest were built by Christian pilgrims from Armenia, the first nation to believe in Christianity. Many churches were built in the Orthodox style of the Byzantine Greeks. Coptic and Ethiopian churches represent the ancient pilgrimage tradition of African Christians. You'll also see medieval Latin Catholic churches from the Crusader era, and churches of the Franciscan Terra Sancta mission. Western-style Anglican, Lutheran, and reformed churches are relative latecomers to Jerusalem.

STATION

II

Such immense diversity in the crowded vicinity of the Via Dolorosa can be bewildering. So bear in mind that this tour is a spiritual journey, not a literal one. We are pilgrims meditating on the significance of the last hours of Jesus Christ. Jesus never walked the stones of today's Via Dolorosa, with or without His cross. Although the roads of the Old City follow the lines of the town built by the Emperor Hadrian after AD 135, they are ten to fifteen feet above the original ones. Furthermore, the first and second stations have no historical basis. The Lithostratus, which you are about to visit, and the Ecce Homo arch were built more than a century after Jesus walked the earth.

So stop for a moment. Try to tune out the present sights and sounds. Engage your imagination and picture a time when only the oldest of these ancient and newer buildings existed and none of them had the religious significance we accord them. Imagine what the Old City looked like in Jesus's day and what life there might have been like.

 **The Second Station**

Across the street from the first station, by the compound of the Franciscan monastery, you'll find the second station of the cross. Head back down the steps from the first station, go left, and look for a marker on your right with the roman numeral II.

The second station is an extension of the first. The buildings here invite you to reflect on the brutality Jesus endured following His condemnation by Pilate up to the moment when He actually picked up the heavy, roughhewn instrument of His own execution. Immediately following Jesus's sentencing,

> the soldiers led Him away into the hall called Praetorium, and they called together the whole garrison. And they clothed Him with purple; and they twisted a crown of thorns, put it on His head, and began to salute Him, "Hail, King of the Jews!" Then they struck Him on the head with a reed and spat on Him; and bowing the knee, they worshiped Him. And when they had mocked Him, they took the purple off Him, put His own clothes on Him, and led Him out to crucify Him.
>
> (MARK 15:16–20)

Visitors to Jerusalem often overlook the Church of Condemnation and the Church of Flagellation. But if you want to know more about the religious history of this city, you should visit these two Roman Catholic churches, which face each other across a courtyard. The compound is administered by the Franciscans, and the adjacent monastery houses an important archaeological museum, the Studium Biblicum Franciscanum, that is well worth visiting.

The striking architecture of the Church of Flagellation, on the right side of the courtyard, dates from 1839, but it was extensively restored between 1927 and 1929 by the Italian Franciscan architect Antonio Barluzzi, who designed many churches in the Holy Land. Visitors are surprised by the beauty and serenity of the building, and many find it spiritually inspiring. The three stained-glass windows show, from left to right, Pontius Pilate washing his hands from sin, Jesus being flogged and a crown of thorns placed on His head, and Barabbas rejoicing at his release.

The second chapel, the Church of Condemnation, is smaller. The Roman stone pavement, or Lithostratos, discovered under this church extends to the nearby Sisters of Zion Convent. The convent was originally held to be the Praetorium where Pilate passed sentence on Jesus.

> [Pilate] brought Jesus out and sat down in the judgment seat in a place that is called The Pavement, but in Hebrew, Gabbatha. Now it was the Preparation Day of the Passover, and about the sixth hour. And he said to the Jews, "Behold your King!"
>
> (JOHN 19:13–14)

The Lithostratos has been dated to the time of Hadrian (AD 117–138), long after Jesus. However, the squares and triangles cut into the stone slabs provide a vivid reminder of the gospel account. They are thought to trace back to the barbaric Game of the King played by Roman soldiers. Selecting one of their prisoners to serve as the "king," the soldiers would outfit him with a robe and a mock crown and scepter. Then, using sheeps' knuckles for dice, they would gamble for all the "king's" possessions. The grand-prize winner won the right to kill the wretched prisoner.

## Carrying the Cross on Tour

Catholic tour groups from around the world want to walk the Via Dolorosa. Each group is led by a priest from their church or parish, who says the required prayers from the liturgy book at every station of the cross.

At the second station, the group is given a large wooden cross in the courtyard of the Flagellation Church, which is usually crowded but provides a great atmosphere. I conduct groups of various sizes, but I make sure everyone in a group gets to carry the cross. Time and again I have watched people's faces change as they connect with the path Jesus may have walked all those years ago.

**As soon as you step outside the Church of the Flagellation courtyard, you'll encounter two Israeli soldiers, armed with rifles, guarding the entrance to the well-known Tunnel Tour.** The tunnel runs along the Western Wall under the streets of the Muslim Quarter and emerges on the site of the former Antonia Fortress, now the Al-Omariyeh school. Almost every tourist interested in archaeology will book a tunnel tour, and the soldiers will accompany every group finishing the Western Wall tunnel tour all the way back to the Jewish Quarter.

Inside the tunnel, you can see ancient Jerusalem from the Second Temple period and other archeological findings. Most importantly, you will find the foundations of the Antonia Fortress that stood here two thousand years ago.

##  The Cross of Humiliation

*"Ma atah oseh po?"* the Israeli soldier demanded of me in Hebrew. "What are you doing here?"

"Nothing," I replied—and the next instant, he was aiming his rifle at me!

The year was 1987, the year the First Intifada began, and I was twelve years old, playing in the streets of the Via Dolorosa, utterly unaware that a riot was underway in the market. But as I was heading home, suddenly soldiers were all around. Some were sitting right at a point I had to pass—and now this one, a man with an ugly reputation, was pointing his gun right at my head!

Click. Click. He pulled the trigger twice.

The magazine was empty. He was just dry-firing, amusing himself at my expense, but I was terrified.

Since my only way home in the Old City lay directly past him, I kept walking as fast as I could, trembling inside and hoping to get by without any further incident.

No such luck. The soldier got up, approached me, and without warning, *smack!* slapped me hard across my face! I began to cry in earnest. I was hurt. I was afraid for my life. And I guess the man realized I had done nothing wrong, because after that, he let me go. I ran home, crying hard.

The slap stung all the more because I hadn't deserved it, and the clicks echoed in my head. My dad, during his years as a policeman, had never slapped me like that, let alone scared me with his gun.

Lest it sound like I'm singling out Israeli soldiers, I assure you that, for a Palestinian Christian, oppression comes from every side. On another occasion, I had finished school at New Gate for the day and gone with my friends to play at Damascus Gate in East Jerusalem, the Muslim section of the city. I was standing near a toy shop opposite the gate when one of the local boys approached me—a big, fat, strong-looking kid.

"Are you Christian or Muslim?" he asked.

With a big smile on my face, I replied, "Christian."

*Wham!* Out of nowhere he hit me in the face. I reeled back in pain and confusion but otherwise did not react. I was too stunned to do anything except, instinctively, turn the other cheek, not realizing I was doing exactly what Jesus said I should do when mistreated (Matt. 5:39). The pain was intense, and I started to cry. *Why did he do that?* I thought. *I did nothing wrong!*

The owner of the toy shop, who happened to be a Christian, saw what had happened. He came out, took my hand, comforted me, and then sent me home.

## ♡ The Countercultural Strength of Forgiveness

How should I have responded to those two incidents? It would have been natural for me to hate the Israeli soldier and strike back at the Muslim bully. I could have allowed unforgiveness to fester inside me through the years, embittering me toward other classes of people just as I myself have been judged for nothing more than my own ethnicity.

But that is not the way of Jesus. He teaches a very different approach:

> "You have heard that it was said, 'An eye for an eye and a tooth for a tooth.' But I tell you not to resist an evil person. But whoever slaps you on your right cheek, turn the other to him also. If anyone wants to sue you and take away your tunic, let him have *your* cloak also. And whoever compels you to go one mile, go with him two. Give to him who asks you, and from him who wants to borrow from you do not turn away." (MATT. 5:38–42)

Commentaries on this passage usually say Jesus is teaching nonretaliation: we Christians are not to seek revenge. That is certainly true. But of course, He could have just said, "Don't hit back"; that's plain language. Instead He says, "Turn the other cheek as well." It seems to me that Jesus is pointing us beyond mere nonretaliation to something more powerful. There is a spiritual significance in turning the other cheek.

In my culture, hitting someone most often happens in the context of marital violence. And probably nine times out of ten, it is the husband who hits his wife. What should she do when that happens—stand there and take it? Is that what Jesus is saying?

I have seen a lot of marital violence, especially in the Old City, where there is no privacy and everyone knows each other's personal stories inside the homes. I know of hundreds of incidents, ranging from a simple bruise on the wrist to spouse rape and even murder. I get so angry when I see this happening!

I don't think Matthew 5:39 is telling us to let someone treat us like a punching bag. However, we also cannot interpret a biblical passage based solely on what we consider common sense. We need to discern the spirit of this passage so we can understand the mind of God.

Out of concern for the other person, the Christian foregoes his or her right to retaliate: "As God forgave me, so I for Christ's sake forgive you. I want you to see and receive the love of God. And ultimately I want you to be saved. That's why I waive my right to retaliate"—because love is the most powerful weapon for winning another person.

And what can be a better expression of love than forgiveness? People can see what kind of Christian you are by how you react to life's circumstances. If you strike back at your abuser, you are acting like any non-Christian. But if you turn the other cheek, you are demonstrating the love God shows to each and every one of us. And if that is what it takes for someone to see God's love, then it is worth another slap. If giving you my coat can help you be saved, then take my coat, please. If walking a second mile can help you be saved, then let me walk a third mile if necessary. That is the attitude of the spiritual man and the mark of a godly Christian walk.

My boyhood experience at Damascus Gate probably convinced the Muslim kid that Christians are weak, stupid, and naive. But I believe that after some years he eventually realized how forgiving I was and that there is power in forgiveness and love. Perhaps that incident opened his eyes to the love of God. To this day I continue praying for that boy, now a grown man like me, that he will accept Christ in his heart.

Being a Christian in Jerusalem is not easy. There is much to forgive, but my Jesus taught me to do so. The world I grew up in can be harsh, and because letting someone push you around is seen as weakness, many find it difficult to understand this level of love that Christ asks us to show the world.

Forgiveness is probably the bravest and hardest thing you and I may ever do.

# ✖ "Ecce Homo"

Leaving the two churches, you turn right through the market and head past some shops. In about ten steps, if you look up you will see, halfway between the second and third stations, one third of an arch with its northern end embedded in the Ecce Homo Church, built in 1868.

This is the central part of the original arch of Ecce Homo (Latin for "Behold the Man"), once part of the Antonia Fortress. According to tradition, this is where Pilate presented Jesus to the crowd:

> Then Jesus came out, wearing the crown of thorns and the purple robe. And Pilate said to them, "Behold the Man!"
>
> (JOHN 19:5)

The arch is in fact a segment of an early Roman triumphal arch with triple openings, erected in AD 135 in honor of Emperor Hadrian's visit. You can find similar arch architecture below the Damascus Gate. These arches represent the main entrances to the city at the time of Hadrian. The Ecce Homo arch was given its present name in the sixteenth century. The site is marked by a relief sculpture above the door of a small Polish chapel, which sits at the junction of the Al-Wad (also known as HaGai) Road.

From here, the Via Dolorosa turns south onto Tariq Bab al-Ghawanima Street and passes the northwestern part of the Temple Mount. Ahead, on the north side of the Via Dolorosa, is the Sisters of Zion Convent, or Notre Dame de Sion Convent.

In Roman times, beyond the Antonia Tower lay the Struthius Pool, a reservoir across which Titus built a ramp for his battering rams during his siege on Jerusalem in AD 68–70. Josephus records that

> after seventeen days of continuous toil the embankments were of vast size. Of the first two, that facing the Antonia was thrown

up by the fifth legion across the pool called Struthius; the other by the twelfth legion about twenty cubits away.[4]

In AD 135 the Struthius Pool was covered over and turned into a cistern by the emperor Hadrian. That cistern may be seen today in the basement of the Notre Dame de Sion Convent, which proudly displays its Hadrianic collection. Hadrian had large flagstones laid on top of the cistern as paving for a market. Wrongly identified as the Lithostratus, these stones are still visible today in the convent and nearby monastery.

This area makes up the east forum of the Roman colony Aelia Capitolina, built on the post-siege ruins of Jerusalem. It was entered through a gateway, the central arch of which was later mistakenly called the Ecce Homo arch.

Close to the Sisters of Zion Convent, the "prison of Christ," where the Lord was purportedly held for questioning, is fabricated. The supposed cell is medieval, and the claim that Jesus was held there dates only from 1911. It competes with another equally bogus "prison of Christ" inside the Church of the Holy Sepulcher.

## ♡ Crown of Suffering, Crown of Glory

Before we move on to station three, step back with me just a couple of paces to the ugly drama enacted just beyond Pilate's Praetorium.

> Now the men who held Jesus mocked Him and beat Him. And having blindfolded Him, they struck Him on the face and asked Him, saying, "Prophesy! Who is the one who struck You?" And many other things they blasphemously spoke against Him.
>
> (LUKE 22:63–65)

> The soldiers twisted a crown of thorns and put it on His head, and they put on Him a purple robe. Then they said, "Hail, King of the Jews!" And they struck Him with their hands.
>
> (JOHN 19:2–3)

What cruel irony! Jesus finally received the words He deserved: "Hail, King of the Jews!" For once He wore a crown upon His head—not a golden crown of sovereignty or an olive crown of victory but a thorny crown of suffering. We can never know the depths of physical pain, the humiliation, or the emotional and spiritual anguish endured by Jesus for us and our salvation.

More important than following Jesus's footsteps from station to station is following His heart and attitude. Paul writes in Philippians 2:5–11,

> Let this mind be in you which was also in Christ Jesus, who, being in the form of God, did not consider it robbery to be equal with God, but made Himself of no reputation, taking the form of a bondservant, and coming in the likeness of men. And being found in appearance as a man, He humbled Himself and became obedient to the point of death, even the death of the cross. Therefore God also has highly exalted Him and given Him the name which is above every name, that at the name of Jesus every knee should bow, of those in heaven, and of those on earth, and of those under the earth, and that every tongue should confess that Jesus Christ is Lord, to the glory of God the Father.

Fellowship with Jesus involves suffering in one form or another (Phil. 3:10). It involves setting aside the urge to retaliate in order to win our enemies with the forgiving love of Christ. It involves serving even those who hurt us by desiring their salvation rather than our getting even.

And let us remember: In Jesus, there is exaltation beyond the suffering, healing beyond the wounding, and sweetness for the bitter cup. In Him, piercing thorns are transformed into a victor's crown.

# ✖ For the Whole World

Continuing down the street, we come to a T-junction. Here in the heart of the Via Dolorosa, where the world's three great mono-theistic religions meet, I usually take my groups to stand on the original stones of Aelia Capitolina near the steps of the Austrian Hospice (hospice here meaning "guest house").

These stones were leveled by the Israeli government in 1967 after some renovations on Al-Wad Street. Standing on Hadrian Street, you can look up to the top of the Austrian Christian Hospice chapel and see a cross. To the left, down Al-Wad Street, an Israeli flag hangs down the side of a building with bulletproof windows. Once the Old City house of former Israeli prime minister Ariel Sharon, the building is inhabited today by Jewish settlers. On its top sits a huge golden menorah, the emblem of the Jewish state. Behind you a mosque stands high, crowned with the crescent sign of the Muslim faith.

At this crossroad, Christianity, Judaism, and Islam jostle each other in a troubled coexistence. But when Jesus walked His per-sonal Via Dolorosa and sacrificed Himself, it was for everyone, not just one particular ethnic group. "For God so loved the world that He gave His only begotten Son, that whoever believes in Him should not perish but have everlasting life" (John 3:16).

■  ■  ■

The sentencing by Pilate is over. The scourging by whip, the pum-meling and cruel mockery of the soldiers, comes to an end; the grueling trip to the place of execution begins. Jesus hoists the coarse crossbeam from which He soon will hang and steels himself for what lies ahead.

The gates of the Antonia Fortress open. The soldiers come out with Jesus and two other condemned prisoners. Jesus is weak and can hardly stand on His own feet. But with great dignity, He emerges from the fortress and begins walking toward Calvary.

––––––––––

*Dear Lord, we so fear humiliation, and we run from suffering. But You chose to take up the cross, a symbol of humiliation and suffering, and You did so with steadfast acceptance. Teach us, as we pray, to carry our burdens with the same grace, remembering that You will never leave or forsake any of us walking our path as refugees in this life.*

# CHAPTER 3

# Jesus Falls
# the First Time

The First Intifada (Palestinian Arab uprising) began suddenly and unexpectedly with a traffic accident on December 8, 1987, at the Erez crossing between Israel and Gaza, where Israeli soldiers check all vehicles with Gazan license plates before they can enter or leave Israel. An Israeli military transport truck crashed into some cars filled with Palestinian workers returning from Israel. Seven Palestinians were injured and four were killed, three of them from the Jabalia refugee camp. And Palestinian anger, long suppressed, finally boiled over.

The largest of eight camps in the Gaza Strip, Jabalia houses almost one hundred and ten thousand Palestinians in less than one square mile (1.4 kilometers). They are descendants of the seventy-eight thousand Palestinians driven from their homes either by force or by fear during the 1948 war that created the State of Israel. Initiating in overcrowded Jabalia, the Palestinian reaction to the 1987 accident spread quickly from Gaza to the West Bank and beyond to all the Palestinian villages and even to Jerusalem.

Both the Palestinian and the Jewish people have known oppression and hardship. Injustice overlooks no nationality. As Palestinian Maronite Christians, I and my ancestors have experienced it at the hands of both Israelis and other Palestinians.

How well Jesus understands! He suffered at the hands of both His own people and the Romans so that they, and you and I, and people of all nations and ethnic groups, might have peace with God, peace in our hearts, peace with each other, and eternal life. On the unforgiving stones of His personal Via Dolorosa, Jesus fell beneath the weight of the cross so that you and I might rise.

##  The Third Station

On the corner of Via Dolorosa and Al-Wad Street, you'll find a stone tablet depicting Jesus's first fall while carrying his heavy cross. The Gospels do not record such an incident; this third station was added by the Crusaders, who designed the route of the Via Dolorosa to emphasize Jesus's humanity—the suffering and exhaustion of the Son of Man.

The Dom Polski Polish church is on the right side of the third station, and the Austrian Hospice is to the left. In 1948 the hospice served as a British military hospital, and then later as a Jordanian one until 1967. Today it is a guest house and a superb coffee shop, well worth visiting. This is a busy junction of several Old City streets, and at least three Israeli soldiers are always posted here. Their primary purpose is to protect Jews who take the shortcut through the Muslim Quarter on their way to pray at the Western Wall.

You can also see a small Byzantine church built during the fifteenth century by Armenian Catholics. The front of it was built into what was originally a twelfth-century entrance to the Hamam el-Sultan Turkish bath; the three arches once formed a porch to the bathhouse. In 1856, the Armenians bought the property leading to the abandoned baths and built their church. In 1947–48 its renovation was financed by a collection taken up by Polish soldiers.

The doorway above the third and fourth stations features a sculptured pediment by the nineteenth-century Italian ceramicist Angelo Minghetti. The entrance area contains part of a column that, according to tradition, was near where Jesus fell. The painting in the entrance hall depicts Him falling under the weight of the cross while angels watch and pray.

Stepping inside through the two iron doors, you will pass through a gift shop, go down some stairs, and reach the chapel of the third station in the crypt of the Polish church. Around the walls are paintings of the way of the cross. Next door is the Armenian Catholic Patriarchate.

# Flight of a Refugee Family

During the mid nineteenth century, mounting tension between Maronite Christians and the Druze (Arab followers of a sect similar to Islam) culminated in persecution of the Maronites by the Druze, causing my ancestors to flee Lebanon. The backstory is as follows.

In 1842 the supreme powers in Constantinople, concerned that Lebanon had gone too far in its separatist policy, partitioned the country between the Maronites and the Druze, following the principle of divide and conquer. The Maronites, who actively embraced the educational and cultural influences of the West, became disproportionately influential in financial and state affairs and soon outdistanced the Druze economically and socially. They also started to establish themselves in districts that had previously been dominated by the Druze.

Tensions simmered between the two groups until finally, in 1860, violence swept the country. More than eleven thousand Maronite Christians were killed by their Druze neighbors, and many of their buildings were torched. That same year my grandfather's family moved to the ancient port city of Jaffa in Ottoman-ruled Palestine. By 1867, eight years later, about one thousand of Jaffa's five thousand inhabitants were Christians; the rest were Arabic-speaking Muslims and Arabic-speaking Jews who had coexisted peacefully for many years. Known as "The Bride of Palestine," Jaffa was a hub of activity, linking the people of Palestine with other port cities around the Mediterranean and the western world.

My father was born in Jaffa, which today is a part of modern Tel Aviv. He told me many stories about his parents' beautiful home in the neighborhood of Ajami, where his family lived until the 1948 war forced them to flee to Egypt. On that day he had no time to gather his clothes, his toys, or even his beloved collection of stamps from all around the world. His parents, thinking the war would end quickly, left everything in their home. They took only the house keys with them, expecting to return in a week or two and resume life as normal.

But there was no returning. Jaffa had become part of the new Jewish state of Israel, and Palestinian refugees—which my father's family now were—were not allowed to reenter Israel. The Israeli government gave the abandoned Arab houses to Jewish immigrants at no cost.

## Back Home from Egypt

The two weeks away from home became twenty years living in an Egyptian town called Shubra. My father, Joseph, went to a Catholic high school, where he learned Italian and French. He passed his teenage years in Shubra until 1964, when the war seemed to quiet down. In that year my grandfather, Anton, decided to bring the family back to their native country.

Between 1948 and 1967, Palestinian Arabs could move freely and settle in the Arab areas controlled by the Hashemite Kingdom of Jordan. These included the West Bank—especially popular cities like Bethlehem, Nablus, Ramallah, and Jericho—and Arab-controlled Jerusalem. During these years, the entire Old City and what is now known as East Jerusalem were controlled by Jordan, which accorded special entry permission to Palestinian refugees who had fled to surrounding Arab countries. So my father's family had no problem moving to the Arab Jordanian part of Jerusalem.

They moved to a neighborhood near Jerusalem's Old City, on the Jordanian side, and for three years they once again enjoyed a normal life. Then in June 1967, the momentous Six Day War broke out. Israeli soldiers captured the east side of Jerusalem, including the Old City, and reunited the whole city under Jewish control.

According to my father, everyone knew war would break out, and this time his family decided not to run away. They were tired of having to rebuild their lives, moving from one place to another. Thus, when the Israelis forced the Jordanian Army out of Jerusalem and the West Bank, my father's family found themselves living under State of Israel rule.

So it was that my father and mother met, married, and raised my three brothers and me in Jerusalem, and that I grew up in a home overlooking the Via Dolorosa and passed through grade school and high school in the Old City.

### Blessing at the Bus Stop

For the apostle Peter, the miracle coin came out of a fish's mouth (Matt. 17:24–27). For me, it lay on the sidewalk.

After graduating from high school, I took a job as a waiter at the American Colony Hotel in East Jerusalem. Three months later, observing my drive and work ethic, the management made me a barman. During my six months in this position, I enrolled to study business administration at Bethlehem University.

Often I would finish work as late as 3:00 a.m., go home to the Old City to sleep for a couple of hours, and then wake up and head to Bethlehem for my university lectures. I was sleepy most of the time, but I had to work hard to pay for my education.

One morning I was completely broke—no money even for fare to ride the special blue bus that took students from the Damascus Gate to Bethlehem. The ticket cost three shekels, just under a dollar, but I did not want to request even this small amount from my dad; he was not working, and our family had no money to spare. But I *had* to get to the university because I had an important exam.

I left my house and walked through the Christian Quarter toward the bus stop, moved by faith but consumed with worry. I couldn't miss that exam. As I walked, I kept praying, "Lord, help me!"

The students were getting on the bus as I arrived. It would pull out shortly. I said, "Lord, I do not want to miss my exam!" I was at the point of tears.

And that's when I saw it—something shiny lying on the ground. I picked it up, cleaned it, and saw that I held a ten-shekel coin!

I was ecstatic! Wiping the tears from my eyes with my dirty hand, I ran to catch the moving bus. Not only could I make it to the university and take my exam, but I could also return to Jerusalem and go to work, and I could even buy a falafel sandwich for three shekels for lunch. Ten shekels was plenty of money for the day. Thank you, Lord!

##  Glimmers of Grace

The third station of the cross reminds us that life is punctuated with down experiences, some of them fleeting and small, some terrible and prolonged. Yet in their midst there is help from above. For Jesus, it was the strength He needed to get up and continue toward His great sacrifice and surpassing triumph. For me, it was a coin glinting in the sun.

Our ups and downs don't necessarily occur in a series, now up and now down. Often we experience both blessings and difficulties at the same time; we stand with one foot on a mountaintop and the other in a valley. But there are times when the valleys are seemingly endless and all-consuming. If that is your experience right now, look around you amid your circumstances. Perhaps you will discover a silver coin of God's grace, too muddy to be instantly recognized for what it is but with the potential to get you where you need to go. That may not be where you expect, but it will be in the center of God's redemptive purpose for your life.

## 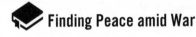 Finding Peace amid War

My first and second years at university, when I was in my late teens, were marred by constant riots and clashes between stone-throwing students and Israeli soldiers. These were the days of the First Intifada, which lasted nearly seven years until Israel and the Palestinians signed the peace agreement known as the Oslo Accords in 1993.

During the worst episode, on a day when riots broke out all over the West Bank, Israeli armed forces parked a huge tank outside the main gate and fired tear gas cylinders through the windows into the classrooms of Bethlehem University. Everywhere you turned, people were passed out on the floor or struggling for breath. At one point I had to jump from a high window and run to safety with a friend, who got shot in the leg by a sniper standing on top of a telephone box. We hid until all was quiet and the army, deciding it had made its point, retreated.

Such violent conflicts were the norm during my studies. I hated university life. I couldn't see a future, I felt depressed, and I wondered if any of it was worth the effort. And then one day . . .

## Alive for the First Time

The riots had started again as usual when I entered the university cafeteria and spotted a group of students holding hands and praying. I was shocked. "What are you doing?" I said. "Run away. No one is here." But they just closed their eyes and continued to pray.

I decided to leave those crazy people by themselves. They were clearly praying in the wrong circumstances.

Yet day after day, whenever I entered the cafeteria, I saw these same students gathering at the same spot. And the amazing thing was, they were *happy*. Their eyes were full of joy. I had never seen students like them before. "These people are weird," I thought. "Chaos and danger are all around, stress is high, exams are tough— and still they are happy." Their attitude was so different from the anger and depression that was all around me.

So one day, out of curiosity, I gathered my courage and asked if I could join them. They welcomed me immediately. There were six of them, boys and girls, and the girls were so beautiful. They were from Gaza, they said. That surprised me. Gaza had become the symbol for the First Intifada, and students from Gaza were the most active in the riots.

"I've been watching you for several months now," I said. "You're always so happy. What's the secret?"

One of the girls replied, "We're Christians." She had the most beautiful blue eyes; I couldn't help staring at them. "I am a Christian too," I said, "but I am never happy like you. If there is something more than what I know, please tell me."

"You have to accept the Lord Jesus Christ in your heart, and the Holy Spirit will enter your life. He will change the past and renew your life. You will become a new person, washed in the blood of Jesus."

"I want that for my life," I said.

They called over one of the guys, who just happened to be a neighbor of mine in the Christian Quarter. He took me to an empty room and we sat down. He said, "Repeat these simple words after me: Jesus Christ, I invite you to enter my life. I surrender everything to you. Forgive me for my sins and come and wash me with Your blood. Holy Spirit, I invite You to live inside me."

It was the shortest prayer I had ever made, but when I had finished I felt complete peace and love in my soul. I felt so safe and happy! It was the Holy Spirit living inside me, but I did not realize it at the time.

I had to tell my twin brother, Tony. Jesus had changed my life! I was joyful and shining, and he needed to have this too.

Tony was skeptical. He said I had become a born-again Christian and figured I'd been brainwashed. In the Middle East, American churches try to influence traditional Christians to turn from their faith to new religions, even cults. So he refused to talk to me.

But I was so full of joy that I did not care. I joined my new fellow Christians almost every day, hanging out with them. And I asked my neighbor to speak to Tony as he had spoken to me. He did—and my twin brother also became a different person in the Lord Jesus Christ and immediately began to change.

■   ■   ■

During one of our weekly prayer meetings at the university, the usual riots broke out. I wanted to leave, but something glued me in place and I could not move. The Holy Spirit pushed on my heart to kneel in the middle of the group and pray for the Israeli soldiers who were shooting bullets at my friends, and to forgive the soldiers, forgive my enemy.

It was so hard for me. I had hated these soldiers all my life because of what they had done to my friends, what I had experienced from them at their checkpoints, and how they had often humiliated me, stopping and searching me so many times for no reason. But I began to cry, "Lord, forgive them." I knew it was the work of the Holy Spirit. Now, instead of throwing stones at the soldiers, I was down on my knees praying for them to have the same joy I had and to experience the same love of Christ in their lives that I knew.

## Growing in Life and Faith

The temptations involved in my job as a barman wore at me constantly. So after praying about it, with no idea how I would survive without an income, I decided to quit the job on faith. My manager's response was to promote me to receptionist—a much better position!

The staff at the American Colony were amazed at how quickly I had advanced. During my next eighteen months at reception, I enjoyed meeting business people, diplomats, and journalists from all over the world. The position fit me beautifully. And I grew in my faith, developing a deeper relationship with the Lord.

I decided to study the Hebrew language and registered in an *ulpan*, a Hebrew language school, for three months. The course was easy for me because Arabic, my mother tongue, is a Semitic language and a sister language to Hebrew. I did not study at all, yet I was one of the best students in the class.

I loved learning a new language, and the hotel security guard, a friend of mine, was fluent in Hebrew. So when I finished my shift at 11:00 p.m., I would wait for him and we would walk back to our homes in the Christian Quarter together, practicing Hebrew all the way. We would arrive at the Damascus Gate close to midnight—two stupid fellows passing through the heart of the Muslim Quarter during the worst days of the Intifada, speaking Hebrew!

One night three men suddenly ran past us, their faces masked by black-and-white *kuffiyehs*. Shortly after, we heard five gunshots. My friend and I immediately switched to Arabic. And suddenly the same men ran by us again in the other direction, shouting, "Run!"

Obviously something serious had happened. I was so scared that I ran all the way home and slammed the door closed. Seconds later I heard the footsteps of the police and the army running by. They had just missed me.

The next day I learned that a Jew had been killed near the steps leading to the Christian Quarter. I went to the university garden to be alone. If those Arab terrorists had overheard my friend and me speaking in Hebrew, they might have shot us too. God protected us that night. I told no one but kept the incident in my heart.

■　■　■

With my financial situation improving, Tony and I made down payments on two adjacent houses in Bir Nabala, an Arab village fifteen minutes northeast of Jerusalem. Given our unstable family background as refugees, we wanted to secure our future. It meant a lot to me to own my own house. In the Middle East we feel connected to our homes and land and families; these biblical values are engraved deeply in our souls, along with the early church's rich concern for community.

During this time the Lord enabled me to leave the American Colony Hotel and work full time in ministry plus two nights a week as watchman at the Christ Church guest house inside Jaffa Gate. For five years I worked hard to pay down the mortgage. And then financial calamity hit, riding on the wings of the Second Intifada.

## The Fall of a Dream

The Palestinian Arab violence known as the Al-Aqsa Intifada, or the Second Intifada, began at the end of September 2000, and no one can say exactly when it ended, though some maintain it was in February 2005. It claimed almost five thousand Palestinian Arab casualties (not counting the almost six hundred killed in intra-Palestinian fighting) and more than one thousand Israeli casualties.

The economy of the West Bank and Gaza was ruined by Israeli incursions and security measures, by the restrictions on Palestinians working in Israel, and by the Palestinians diverting their infrastructure and resources to arms purchases and manufacture. The Separation Barrier—the Israeli security fence built to stop terror attacks—has disrupted Palestinian life in the West Bank ever since. Palestinians carrying explosives are still caught regularly at internal checkpoints.

Large numbers of Israelis who had come to believe in the possibility of peace with the Palestinians felt betrayed by the Second Intifada. Personal friendships between Israelis and Palestinians fell apart. And my five years of paying for a home of my own evaporated in the single day and night it took the Israelis to build their wall separating Bir Nabala from Jerusalem. No longer could I drive to my house in fifteen minutes; now I had to take a two-hour route. I effectively lost my home to the Separation Barrier.

I felt so broken. All the time, work, and money I had invested— all my dreams for the future—gone in twenty-four hours.

## ♡ Get Up and Keep Going!

Weakened by loss of blood and the effort of carrying His cross, Jesus staggered and fell beneath its weight.

There are times in life when we too stumble beneath whatever burden it is we are carrying. The weight of it is too much for us; it drives us to the ground. But every walk with God imposes its load of difficulties. Jesus rose and walked on, and so must we. Whether our fall involves our career, our marriage, our finances, our health, or in my case, my home—whatever dream we have lost, whatever loss drives us to our knees on life's hard pavement—we must rise up in faith and continue on. More is at stake than we know, and our lives, broken and weak though they may be, are of great consequence.

Take courage and fix your eyes on Jesus, "who for the joy that was set before Him endured the cross" (Heb. 12:2). Rise up again and continue on. Life may not be easy, but there is great reward when you get back up and keep walking.

———

*Dear Lord, forgive me when I let fear get in the way of my relationship with You. Forgive me for the times I have fallen short because I've been afraid. You promise provision and protection. Forgive me for failing to trust you when You've proven Yourself to be completely worthy of my trust. Lord! Father, bring hope and faith and a relief from fear, despair, and grief over my losses.*

# CHAPTER 4

# Jesus Meets
# His Mother

Who can fathom the grief of Mary, Jesus's mother, as she watched her firstborn son, battered by Roman soldiers and shredded by the whip, carrying the cross on the way to His execution? Standing at the wayside, how could she not remember moment after moment of her life with Him—His birth at Bethlehem amid the trying conditions of the Roman census. His laughter as He played with other children in the streets of Nazareth. His aptitude and patience as He learned carpentry from His earthly father, Joseph. Her quiet pride as she watched Him assume the trade on His own as a young man.

STATION

**IV**

Yet there were other memories as well, haunting ones that centered on His true identity and mission. Mary thought back to her relief at finding her twelve-year-old in the midst of the teachers in the Jerusalem temple after He had gone missing, and His odd response (Luke 2:41–51). She recalled His family's and her own concern for His sanity (Mark 3:21, 31–32). And with a pang, she could hear, echoing over the broad course of their intertwined lives as mother and son, the old man's prophecy spoken over the child on the day of His dedication:

> Simeon blessed them, and said to Mary His mother, "Behold, this Child is destined for the fall and rising of many in Israel, and for a sign which will be spoken against (yes, a sword will pierce through your own soul also), that the thoughts of many hearts may be revealed." (LUKE 2:34–35)

At the fourth station of the cross, we picture Mary, weaving amid the crowd, desperately seeking every possible glimpse of her son. And now at last there is an opening, and Mary breaks through and locks tearful eyes with her boy. Her baby. Her beloved child.

## ✝ The Fourth Station

The fourth station of the cross is located with the third station and is commemorated with it. They were combined in 2008 to make it easier for pilgrims to pray. Before then it was situated twenty-five meters (eighty feet) farther down Al-Wad Street, but it was hard for pilgrims to stop in the middle of this fast-paced, noisy main route through the Old City. It is full of distractions. A tractor towing a wagon of rolled-up rugs roars past. Egg crates and garbage sacks lie in the street where someone has stacked them. On the corner next to a small trolley, you see a man selling ring-shaped Arab bread rolls called *kaaek*. "One dollar!" he cries.

Yet here amid the modern clamor, this ancient pavement holds memories of centuries past. Named after the Arabic word for "deep valley," Al-Wad Street follows the once deep ravine of the ancient Tyropean Valley, which cuts through the middle of the Old City from Damascus Gate to Dung Gate, separating the Temple Mount from Mount Zion.

The Armenian Church of Our Lady of the Spasm, commemorating Mary's intense grief, sits behind the walls at the fourth station. Excavations in 1874 revealed the remains of a Crusader church on that location, and when the Armenian chapel began to be built in 1881, foundation holes indicated that an even earlier Byzantine church had once stood there. In its crypt, a remarkable fifth-century mosaic was exposed, including the outline of a pair of sandals, said to have been Mary's.

In 1483, Felix Fabri, a Dominican priest and pilgrim, called the ruin The Church of St. Mary at the Swoon. The place was considered holy, and Fabri reported a Crusader-era tradition that every attempt to build on it had been mysteriously destroyed. No one could even remove stones from the rubble.

■  ■  ■

If you continue down to the south of Al-Wad Street, you will reach the Western Wall, which supports the Temple Mount platform where Solomon's Temple (the First Temple) once stood in about 1000 BC. The temple was destroyed four hundred years later by the Babylonians but was reconstructed in 516 BC by Jews returning from exile in Babylon. It was greatly extended and embellished after 19 BC by King Herod. But in AD 70 the Romans destroyed this Second Temple—as Jesus had predicted—when they besieged Jerusalem and ruthlessly crushed a Jewish rebellion.

The massive rock on the Temple Mount is where Abraham prepared to sacrifice Isaac, according to Jewish Tradition, or Ishmael, according to Muslim. In Arabic, the Temple Mount area is known as Alharam Alshareif ("The Noble Sanctuary"). This rock is now covered by the Muslim Dome of the Rock shrine. It is also said to be the rock on which Muhammad alighted on his horse Al-Buraq on his alleged night journey from Mecca and back.

## ♡ Lessons from the Farm

"We Christians are strong like the olive tree. We will never die. We bring life and belong to the land."

My mother's father, Bajes Shaheen, was walking with me, holding my small hand in his old one that had been weathered by many years of working the terraces of his farm at Ein Areek village in the West Bank.

"We will be here forever, never shaken by the wind or the storms," he told me.

It was his way of saying, "Stay in this land."

Indeed, his family had deep roots in the land. The Shaheens were one of five Christian families who founded nearby Ramallah, "The Mountain of God," some five hundred years ago. They were a large family, well known in this area where Muslims and Christians live peacefully together. Here in Ein Areek, where natural springs run through the Palestinian village and pour into a large, lush valley full of fruit trees, my grandfather had worked the earth and raised his children. He knew all about the strength of olive trees, for his own extended family, Roman Catholic Palestinians, owned many profitable olive trees and almost half the land in the village.

My grandfather taught me about the land. He showed me how to build and maintain the stone terraces that are characteristic of the Palestinian landscape. They prevent soil erosion, retain water, and make cultivation easier for the farmers. Today, however, people who can build them are not easy to find. Building terraces is a simple practice but a vanishing one, because of course you have to learn it before you can do it. And both the learning and the doing take a community.

This is so biblical. You cannot build terraces by yourself, just as a Christian cannot stand alone. We need each other; we are a body whose different parts are all joined together and are dependent on one another (1 Cor. 12:12–27).

In the West, the sense of community has been displaced by individualism. It is all about "me and mine." Christians need to rediscover what it means to think as a community.

■ ■ ■

My grandfather used to rise early in the morning to prune his vineyard. Vineyards are a prominent theme in the Bible. Isaiah the prophet likened Israel to a vineyard planted on a fertile hillside (Isa. 5:1–5). Jesus also used the vineyard metaphor: He is the true vine, we are the branches, and the Father is the farmer (John 15:1–8). A farmer's job is to create the best conditions for the vineyard to produce the fruit it is meant to produce. He prunes the branches to enhance their fruitfulness.

He also employs special techniques to preserve moisture in the soil for rain-fed summer crops. At least, that is what farmers used to do. Like terrace building, the techniques and the terms are getting lost to the point that even people working in agriculture no longer know them. But in my grandfather's day, every farmer knew the terms, and how to prepare the land, and especially why. They knew how to plow the soil using the technique called *shaqqa farkha*, in which you open the soil by plowing a trench and then cover it again in another line, thus keeping the soil protected from the sun. This way it doesn't lose its moisture but stays at the right temperature for the seeds to germinate and grow strong and healthy.

God calls us to be a fertile hillside producing good fruit. May the harvest please Him, the Farmer!

## My Mother's Love

My mother, Reema Bajes Shaheen, once told me the story of a neighbor whose baby had beautiful blue eyes, very rare for Arabs. Many people visited this child and envied his blue eyes. But after three months, he became blind. People believed jealous women had put a curse on him, a practice in the Middle East known as the "evil eye." So my mother was extremely protective of my twin and me. We were adorable little children, and so, fearing that someone might put the evil eye on us in similar fashion, she put us in the bedroom when guests visited. Only our family and close friends got to see us when we were babies.

I lived with my mother until my wedding day, as is the custom in our culture. It is considered shameful for a young unmarried man to leave his family's home and live alone. My mother saw me every day and every night. She took care of all my needs—laundry, meals, cleaning, even a cup of Arab coffee or strong tea when I woke up. She prepared breakfast, lunch, and dinner every single day for me and my three brothers. Like every mother, she spoiled her sons!

My mother was excited to see me working hard to purchase a home. And when I bought my house in Bir Nabala, a Palestinian village, she was very proud that I would settle down in a neighborhood so close to her ancestral home.

Imagine, then, how heartbroken she felt when Tony and I lost our houses in Bir Nabala. At first she did not know, but a mother can feel her son's heart and knows when he is happy and when he is in distress. I had not slept even one night in my Bir Nabala house because I was not yet married, and now I never would sleep there. My mother could not bear to see me so despondent and tried in every possible way to help. She was a mother who loved her son, knew her son, and always stood by him.

My neighbors all followed the story, and when I came home late from work, I would find them with tears in their eyes because of my great loss. But the person most deeply grieved was my beloved mother. The dream her son had worked so hard for had been lost, his future security shattered, and my mother was speechless. She had no words to console me, only a mother's tears. But they spoke of her love for me as no words could.

## ♡ Tradition and Truth

When you visit the stations of the cross, you will relate readily to seven of the scenes, those that are clearly based on the Bible. The other half seem odd because they depict nonbiblical events, including three falls of Jesus and the encounters between Jesus and His mother and Jesus and Veronica. These were not derived from Scripture; they are ancient church traditions. I find tradition helpful, but Scripture is our primary source of spiritual truth.

Pope John Paul II seems to have shared this concern about the lack of biblical foundation for the traditional stations of the cross, though he observed them without hesitation. In 1991, he instituted a new series of fourteen stations of the cross, each based solely on Scripture. (See appendix E for a comparison of the traditional stations with the 1991 papal revision.)

Yet regardless of whether Mary's grief is mentioned in the scriptural record, there is no question it was as agonizing as the long-ago prophecy spoken about her child had predicted. Let us take time, at this fourth station of the cross, to imagine the drama that might have played out as the sword pierced her motherly heart.

## A Mother's Broken Heart

Mary tries to get closer to speak a word to her son. Jesus looks up at her. He sees her and wants to comfort her. He has known her tender love for many years, her constant care and loving heart. Their eyes meet. He does not say a word but looks straight at His mother. They communicate through their eyes, and He strengthens her soul. In His heart, Jesus is repeating His words to her when He was twelve: "Did you not know that I must be about my Father's business?" (Luke 2:49).

Mary remembers her own response to the angel Gabriel at the annunciation: "Behold the handmaid of the Lord" (Luke 1:38 KJV). She has never failed to be His handmaid on whose absolute faithfulness God could rely.

All this transpires in one or two brief seconds. Then Jesus is roughly pushed ahead by the soldiers. There is no time for talk; He must keep moving.

■　■　■

For me, losing my home was a terrible cross; for my mother, as with Mary, that cross was a sword that pierced her own heart—for my mother loved me, and my pain was her pain.

We live in an unfair world, and in Jerusalem the Christian community suffers a great deal daily. People think we are weak because when we face confrontations with Jews and Muslims, we withdraw. But Jesus sacrificed Himself not because He was weak but because He had great love in His heart, and that love made Him strong.

We, your brothers and sisters in the Middle East, sacrifice ourselves almost every day because we want to be ambassadors of God's love on earth and reflect Jesus in our lives. Although we are a minority, we contribute greatly to the transformation of many lives. Remember us—for we desire to serve the world as Christ would have us do, bringing change to our neighborhood and our society. The price we pay is often costly, not only to us but also to those who love us.

Perhaps you, like Jesus's mother, feel grief over someone you love who has suffered an injustice or bears a deep wound of one kind or another. Whether you are a mother or father, wife or husband, sibling or friend, you feel the thrust of Mary's sword in your own heart. May God strengthen you, comfort you, and help you, in the Spirit of His Son, to bear the cost on behalf of His kingdom.

———

*Lord, a sword of sorrow pierced the loving heart of your mother, Mary. We pray for all the wounded mothers in the Middle East and in the whole world who behold their sons and daughters suffering and dying in front of them and can do nothing to help. Lord, have mercy on those mothers. Have compassion on them and heal their hearts.*

*Lord, grant that we who look back on Mary's sorrows with compassion might receive the healing fruits of your sufferings.*

# CHAPTER 5

# Simon of Cyrene Helps Jesus Carry His Cross

I t wasn't a journey he'd made lightly. One didn't walk a thousand miles and then back again on a whim, even under the best of conditions. And the journey from Cyrene to Jerusalem was *not* the best of conditions. Between the small Greek colony on the northeast coast of present-day Libya and Jerusalem lay a long stretch of rugged terrain with harsh, changeable weather, fierce wild animals, and, perhaps most dangerous of all, bandits who would cheerfully leave a traveler's bones to bleach in the desert.

STATION

V

Nevertheless, every Jew yearned to celebrate the Passover in Jerusalem, even if only once or twice in a lifetime for those who lived afar. So Simon had made the month-long trek, and he had arrived, safe but tired. The many days of walking under the hot sun had taxed his energy. His heart felt glad to be here, but his body wanted to rest.

But rest was not what lay in store for Simon of Cyrene on this day. For this man who had expended himself traveling the long, dangerous distance from his hometown to Jerusalem, God had

ordained a singular reward: an unforgettable role in the greatest
Passover of all.

##  The Fifth Station

Leaving the Armenian church, we turn left through Al-Wad Street,
passing shops that sell all kinds of decorative women's religious
clothing, and head to the famed Abu Shukri—the best hummus
restaurant in all Jerusalem. I take most of my tourists here for
lunch to enjoy a cultural experience. Order a bowl of hummus,
some falafel balls and pickles, and have a cup of mint tea; this will
be the most authentic and tastiest hummus meal you'll ever enjoy!

**The fifth station is just beyond this well-known restaurant,
on the corner of the Via Dolorosa and Al-Wad Street. The road
turns sharply to the right and starts climbing up the hill in a
series of stairs. Here the way of the cross begins the ascent toward
Golgotha.**

A small Franciscan chapel dedicated to Simon the Cyrenian is located at this station. The doorkeeper is my neighbor from the Christian Quarter and another Palestinian Christian. On most days he stands there to welcome tourists and open the chapel for them.

This chapel was established in 1229 as the Franciscans' first site in Jerusalem. A cavity in a square stone on the right side of the chapel is said to be an imprint of Jesus's hand. According to tradition, when Simon helped Jesus with His cross, Jesus placed His hand on this stone to steady Himself. Thus the stone became revered, and countless thousands of people touching it over the centuries have smoothed its surface. In reality, any stone Jesus actually touched would be ten to fifteen feet below the present street level.

But again, our pilgrimage along the Via Dolorosa is spiritual, not physical. Allow this fifth station to carry you back to one man's deeply personal experience with the cross of Christ as he took it on his own shoulders in the most literal sense.

## ♡ Who Was Simon?

> They compelled a certain man, Simon a Cyrenian, the father of Alexander and Rufus, as he was coming out of the country and passing by, to bear His cross.          (MARK 15:21)

What a shock it must have been for Simon, after completing his month-long journey from Cyrene to Jerusalem, to find himself forced by the Roman soldiers to carry the cross of a condemned man!

Cyrene, now modern Shahhat, Libya, was founded as a Greek colony in the seventh century BC and became a Roman province in 74 BC. By the first century, a large number of Jews lived in Cyrene and are referred to in connection with early Christianity.

According to Acts 6:9, Cyrenian Jews had a synagogue in Jerusalem. Simon was probably visiting Jerusalem for the Passover, but we are told little about him.

However, his sons Alexander and Rufus were apparently known to the readers of Mark's gospel (Mark 15:21). And in 1941, when the land that is now Israel was ruled under the British Mandate, two archaeologists made a surprising discovery in the Kidron Valley. Among ten ancient ossuaries—burial boxes containing the bones of a deceased person—was a simple stone box from the first century bearing the inscription "Alexander son of Simon." Whether the reference is to *the* Alexander and *the* Simon cannot be proved; nevertheless, the finding is a striking one and fits flawlessly with the biblical text.

There are three other biblical references to Cyrene:

- Jews from the district around Cyrene were present in Jerusalem on the day of Pentecost (Acts 2:10).
- Men from Cyprus and Cyrene were responsible for the first sermons delivered to the gentiles at Syrian Antioch (Acts 11:20).
- Lucius of Cyrene was one of the prophets or teachers at Antioch (Acts 13:1).

As for Simon himself, we can piece together a reasonable picture of how his part in the gospel account may have unfolded. He probably stayed the night before in the countryside. On his way into the city, he came across a procession—involving what, he had no idea. Drawing closer, he was shocked to see a badly beaten man stumbling under the weight of a heavy cross, on His way to be crucified.

It's unlikely that Simon knew anything about Jesus before this encounter. But suddenly he found himself pressed into service as the Roman soldiers, recognizing that their prisoner was too weak to carry the cross any farther, grabbed Simon out of the crowd and ordered him to carry it. So it was that Simon, newly arrived from his long journey, found himself bearing the instrument of Jesus's execution, easing the physical burden of the One who was taking the whole of fallen humanity's spiritual burden on Himself.

 ## Tony, My Cross Bearer

How we need people in our lives to carry our crosses when the load gets too much for us! One of my chief cross bearers has been my twin brother, Tony. When the troubles of living in Jerusalem, the conflicts and hostility, the responsibilities, even the problems I have sometimes caused for myself bore me down, Tony has stood with me—every time. Being a tour guide takes all my energy, and there have been times when I just wanted to quit. But when I was exhausted, Tony would step in and take the tour from me until I had rested. Thanks to him, I could come back stronger and continue on my path, my vocation, as a guide.

Mine is not an easy job in Israel and Palestine. We minority Palestinian Christians are not recognized in the travel business; the biggest travel agents are the Israeli Jews or, in Palestine, the Muslims. They control the industry and attract most tour groups from outside the country. Twins Tours is one of the few Spirit-filled evangelical agencies servicing church groups in Israel and Palestine. As a small Christian-family agency, we fall between the cracks. But the harder it gets, the more blessed and anointed our tours become. It is as Zechariah 4:6 says: "'Not by might nor by power, but by My Spirit,' says the LORD of hosts."

### Tales of Two Twins

Tony shoved me roughly to one side and I hit the wall hard.

*What on earth!* I turned to him, shaken and confused. Why did he do that?

Then I saw the heavy bag of cement lying on the pavement where I'd been about to walk. It had fallen from the roof of the construction site we were passing and would have landed smack on my head were it not for my brother's quick action. He had just saved my life!

Tony, my identical twin, has been with me all my life and experienced all the same challenges I had living in this part of the world. We learned to be strong, tough, and aware of what was happening around us, both physically and spiritually. Tony is my partner, my best friend in life; without him, my life would not have become successful.

In 1975, my father and mother were delighted to learn that my mother was pregnant. But with ultrasound unavailable in the Old City, no one, not even the doctor, knew she was carrying twins. My dad figured it out because of her tremendous appetite and because twins occurred regularly in his family line. But my mother thought he was just teasing her.

She learned otherwise the morning of our birth. Tony came first, and while the nurse was checking him over they noticed that my mother's stomach was still big. My dad said, "There is another one inside!" Five minutes later the nurse delivered me from my mother's womb and cut the cord, and now there were two tiny, weak creatures crying with the same tone. According to my mother, I was a reddish color, with a face like a red, shining apple—and I was the louder one.

The whole Moubarak family came to visit, and they helped our parents choose our names, Tony and Andre.

Two years passed, and the time came for us to be circumcised (circumcision then did not immediately follow birth the way it does today). I remember the occasion well, even though I was so young. A Jewish rabbi came to our home. He wore white gloves and carried a weird silver instrument. I knew something bad was going to happen, but I did not know what. Suddenly I heard Tony screaming at the top of his voice. I knew my turn was next. I started to cry even before the rabbi touched me with his weird instrument, because my twin brother was suffering. Soon I was crying because I hurt all on my own! Thus my first experience with a Jewish religious man was painful. I did not know it was for my health and well-being.

■ ■ ■

Because Tony and I looked identical, we were often the center of attention. When our mother wheeled us through the streets of the Old City in a twin stroller, people would stare and often stop us to get a better look. At first I liked the attention; later it grew tiresome, but when you're a twin it eventually becomes normal.

Even our mother mistook us sometimes. As a baby, I was always the first to open my mouth and grab the food during mealtime, and once she fed me twice and Tony not at all! It was not my fault—I never said no to food. Of course, she fixed the problem as soon as she figured it out.

Later, my two younger brothers were born, Albert and then Alfred. The four of us grew up in a tiny house that received little sunlight. We used it mostly for sleeping—my brothers and I all in one room, our beds so close there was hardly any room to move. That was the arrangement until one by one we married and moved out. Today Albert works in the office at Twins Tours & Travel, and my mother lives with him and his family in the village of Beit Fage (the biblical Bethphage) on the Mount of Olives close to Bethany. Alfred lives in French Hill and owns a gift shop in Ein Karem.

■ ■ ■

When my twin and I were about thirteen years old, the Social Affairs Department interviewed us at school as part of a survey they were conducting on twins. Our interviewers were two beautiful Jewish ladies. They separated us, taking Tony to one classroom and me to another.

My interviewer was blonde with blue eyes, and her eyes got my attention. I sat down, staring at them, and she gave me some white paper and colored pencils and asked me to draw whatever I wanted to. I drew a green tree with some blue sky and a couple of birds, the sun, and the soil. (Mostly, I just wanted to look at the lady's beautiful eyes!) Then she gave me forty simple questions to answer—what was my favorite color, who was my best friend, what was my favorite thing to do, and so on.

My brother got the same test, and two weeks later the principal told us the results. Tony and I had given the same answers 98 percent of the time! We had even drawn the same picture—same green tree, birds in the same place in the sky, same color of sunshine. Our drawings were incredible mirror images.

We had so much fun in school as twins! We were kind of famous. But we had different friends, and over the years our personalities started to change. Tony was much smarter than me in class, always studying hard and getting better grades, while I did not like to study and got bored quickly. As a result, Tony passed the GCE exams (general certificate of education, set by Britain) and, exempted from the last year of school, finished a year before me.

I had to study the last year without my twin. That was hard because Tony had helped me a lot. Now I had to do it by myself. I was taught about Shakespeare's *Merchant of Venice*, and about Jean-Jacques Rousseau, and about the French Revolution, but nothing at all about the history of Palestine or Israel. When at last the day came to take the tough final government test, I passed it and was glad to be finished.

## The Twins Go to College

Together, Tony and I enrolled to study business administration at Bethlehem University. That was our best adventure. We were like celebrities, attracting the attention of all the students and the beautiful girls. When we entered the cafeteria—one of the school's few gathering places—all the action would stop and the students would say, "Here are the twins." Some would even point at us. It was kind of embarrassing. I liked the attention, but it got to be a bit much at times, to the point where my brother and I often chose not to walk together.

At first we took the same courses and lectures, and our old study patterns continued, with Tony studying a lot and I studying hardly at all. Again Tony helped me a lot, even switching places with me during exams. I recall one exam in particular. It was a two-hour, multiple-choice exam about microeconomics based on a 250-page book which I hadn't even attempted to read; I preferred to hang out with my friends and play. But my brother did study hard, and I figured I would just cheat off him by switching seats after he had completed his test.

The test day came, and I hadn't a clue, but I trusted my brother. We had agreed that after exactly one hour, one of us would get up to go the toilet, and after a minute, the other would do the same. At the toilets we exchanged our wallets and IDs, and I returned to his chair and he sat in mine and passed the test for me.

What I was doing was wrong, and it became such a habit that Tony finally got fed up and refused to help me anymore. Along came a computer science exam, and once again I was clueless. I begged Tony for his help, but he did not even look at me, and I failed the exam.

So as an act of revenge, I stole one of his girlfriends!

At first, I honestly did not know he was dating her. I was sitting outside the cafeteria when a beautiful girl approached me, said hello as if she knew me, and then started a conversation as if it was the most natural thing in the world. I did not mind at all! I thought she was bold, I liked her personality, and before she left, I had made a date with her. I had no idea she was also dating my twin.

Then after a couple of dates, she said, "Tony, you sound different today. What is wrong?"

Oops!

So she was with Tony and had dated me thinking I was him. Awkward. But I enjoyed the thought of taking revenge on my brother for refusing to help me with my computer science test, so I continued the conversation as if I were Tony.

Two weeks passed, and then suddenly the girl began avoiding me. My ruse had been discovered. So I went to my brother and told him what had happened. He was mad at me—he even said he hated me. He had worked so hard to gain the trust of this girl, and I had ruined it for him.

■  ■  ■

All these shenanigans happened before we became Spirit-filled Christians. We were still searching for the Lord in our lives. But even after we found Him, our identical appearances led to other innocent, funny incidents in church and at work. Everyone thought I would marry first because I was such a schmoozer. I was relieved when my twin married first to a lovely wife and got all the attention. Tony now has two children: Kareen, his daughter, and Joseph, named after his grandfather in accordance with the Arab Christian tradition for naming firstborn sons.

I am so happy for my twin brother and so grateful for him. Many people have helped me carry my cross at different times in my life, but no one more than Tony. When my world seemed to be collapsing around me, when I could not make it on my own, Tony, like Simon of Cyrene, stepped in to take the weight from my shoulders. He learned how to be a tour guide with me. He helped me obtain a good, steady job and made a commitment to stand with me in all aspects of life. And today Tony continues to assist me in the office at Twins Tours & Travel Ltd. When he is not personally guiding a group, he helps connect groups with the right drivers, hotels, and programs.

## ♡ Identifying with Jesus and His Cross

No doubt Simon the Cyrenian felt hesitant about taking up the condemned man's cross. Would he somehow end up sharing Jesus's fate? But he was also afraid to provoke the soldiers, so he did as ordered. "On him they laid the cross that he might bear it after Jesus" (Luke 23:26)—and that's the last we hear of Simon. After that, he disappears from the biblical record.

Yet although Simon appears only momentarily in the Bible, the role he plays in carrying Christ's cross is an intimate one. In a sense he participates in Jesus's crucifixion, and so foreshadows, in a unique way, a profound theological truth expounded on by Paul the apostle: "I have been crucified with Christ; it is no longer I who live, but Christ lives in me; and the life which I now live in the flesh I live by faith in the Son of God, who loved me and gave Himself for me" (Gal. 2:20).

When we put our faith in Christ, we share in His death by dying to sin and to ourselves. Our "old self" is crucified so that we might be set free from committing the same sins again and again, unable to stop. When we repent and accept Jesus's forgiveness, we become alive in Christ, who lives in us through the Holy Spirit. In this sense we can identify with Simon of Cyrene, who found himself participating in the crucifixion of Christ and the way of the cross.

Many people become Christians without really knowing what is involved. We are told about salvation and eternal life, which sound pretty good, but not about servanthood, sacrifice, and death to self. Only later in our Christian walk do we discover that we are expected to be crucified with Christ. Jesus does not force us to follow Him against our will. Rather, He invites us, calls us to take up our cross and follow Him, and in return, He offers us abundant life.

> "If anyone desires to come after Me, let him deny himself, and take up his cross daily, and follow Me. For whoever desires to save his life will lose it, but whoever loses his life for My sake will save it."                                         (LUKE 9:23–24)

---

*Lord, both Simon the Cyrenian and Tony remind me of two important truths: that there are times when I must lovingly help others bear the cross they carry, and that I must take up my own cross and follow You. Help me, Lord, to do these things. Help me carry my cross, letting go of my life so that I can receive the abundant life of Your kingdom. And teach me to come forward whenever someone is crushed by burdens.*

*Teach me how to forget myself and reach out to others who are suffering. Help me to be a voice for those who cannot speak, an eye for those who cannot see, an ear for those who cannot hear. Above all, let me be a heart of love and care in a world full of prejudice and hatred. Let me be a source of light for those who are burdened by darkness. Lead me in my walk with You to discover my calling and vocation in this world.*

# CHAPTER 6

# Veronica Wipes
# the Face of Jesus

Frequently I meet people who are surprised to learn that Christians still live in the Middle East. Some believe Islam has completely replaced Christianity; others assume that today's Arab Christians are the product of relatively recent missionary activity to Arab Muslims. Yet the Christian church was born in this region in notable ancient cities such as Jerusalem, Samaria, Damascus, Antioch, Alexandria, and their surrounding towns and villages. Christian communities here can trace their roots back to the disciples of Jesus and the day of Pentecost. In the Middle Eastern mentality, the sense of time differs from that of westerners. All the centuries coexist and directly affect us today.

The story of Veronica did not originate with us. It does not appear in any of the gospels but arose centuries later as a Roman Catholic western tradition, linked with a veil with which a woman named Veronica is said to have wiped the sweaty, blood-streaked face of Jesus and which thereafter bore His imprint. Yet though Veronica is a legend, the compassion she embodies is real and compelling, and the sixth station of the cross invites us to consider its loving nature and how well we ourselves reflect it.

 ## The Sixth Station

Continuing up the steps from station five, you will see on your left a green door flanked by two big, square stone slabs. This house dates back to the thirteenth century, making it almost seven hundred years old, yet people still live in it. Farther along, beyond an overhead arch, on your left are two arched doors; the first is overlaid with black iron trusses and the second is blue, and between them, an ancient pillar embedded in the wall bears a Latin inscription with the name Veronica.

Tradition has it that here is where Veronica wiped Jesus's face with her veil. The symbolic name Veronica—which combines the Latin words *verus,* meaning "true," and *icon,* meaning "image"—implies that the image of Jesus's face purportedly imprinted on the veil is an authentic icon. Hence the piece of cloth known as the Veil of Veronica became revered by Roman Catholics. The incident is derived from Luke 23:27, which says that "a large number of people followed him, including women who mourned and wailed for him" (NIV).

To the left of the pillar, the front door of the small Chapel of the Holy Face is usually closed. I always ask the nun for permission to take my group inside. The interior is small and cave-like, lit by just a few candles, with a simple stone altar. It is a haven of tranquility compared to the busy street outside. A stone plaque commemorates the visit by Pope Paul VI in 1964.

Built in 1882, the chapel belongs to the Order of Little Sisters of Jesus. During its construction, the remains of two monasteries were discovered. One was a section of the chapel of the Crusader monastery of St. Cosmos, known to have existed in Jerusalem between AD 546 and 563. Also found there were the apparent remains of the Monastery of St. Damian. Saints Cosmos and Damian were brothers, born in Arabia and martyred during the persecutions of the Roman Emperor Diocletian's reign. We know that they were physicians and early church fathers who later became patron saints. The chapel was completely restored and refurbished by Antonio Barluzzi in 1953, including its Crusader arches, and below it is an unlit Crusader crypt.

The blue door on the right of the pillar opens into a shop run by the Little Sisters of Jesus, who sell icons.

■　■　■

The story of Veronica is told not in the Gospels but in early non-canonical writings. A second-century version of the Acts of Pilate says that Veronica (Bernice in the Greek story) was the same woman whom Jesus had healed of a blood disorder (Matt. 9:20–22), and that she came to His trial to assert His innocence. Later fourth- and fifth-century versions say that Veronica possessed a cloth imprinted with the face of Jesus. Western pilgrims carried the story back to Europe. As the stations of the cross developed in late medieval times, Veronica was remembered for wiping the face of Jesus and for having His image on her veil. A healing relic with an image of Jesus's face came to be known as Veronica's Veil, or the *Sudarium* (sweat cloth), and was venerated in St. Peter's Basilica in Rome as early as the eighth century.

## ♡ Insights for Your Heart

The Scriptures never provide a physical description of Jesus. However, they do tell us there was nothing about His looks or His station in life that drew people to Him naturally.

> He had no beauty or majesty to attract us to him, nothing in his appearance that we should desire him. He was despised and rejected by mankind, a man of suffering, and familiar with pain. Like one from whom men hide their faces he was despised, and we held him in low esteem.     (ISA. 53:2–3 NIV)[5]

At the sixth station, we encounter Jesus at the culmination of His rejection by the Jewish leaders, mocked and jostled by the soldiers, struggling toward Golgotha. Amid the crowd, one woman watches and, moved with compassion, decides to do what she can to ease His suffering. Stepping forth from the sideline, Veronica takes her veil and with it wipes the sweaty, grimy, blood-caked face of Jesus.

It is a small gesture, over in a moment—but what might it have meant to Jesus? Amid the cruelty of the soldiers, kindness; amid the unrelenting harshness, a tender hand wiping away the filth, and loving eyes gazing into His own. One small act of great consequence. One person who did *not* despise or reject Him. One heart that cared.

Perhaps Veronica knew Jesus. Perhaps she had once sat listening to His words, and now they echoed in her heart. We can say at least this much, that Veronica reflects a heart that showed compassion to a man when no one else would.

Simon of Cyrene served Jesus by bearing His heavy cross over part of the journey to Golgotha. Veronica, in contrast, stepped forth in a moment with a soft, light cloth and wiped the blood and sweat from Jesus's face. We need both kinds of help and care in our own life—practical, load-bearing help but also quick, empowering doses of kindness, perhaps just a brief prayer or a simple word of encouragement right when we need it most.

## Marie, My Veronica

The girl walking past my vehicle was beautiful like an angel. And the best part was, I knew her! Well . . . kind of.

It was 10:15 on a calm evening in November 2005, and I was about to park my car in the Christ Church compound at Jaffa Gate after attending a family obligation with my mother. The two of us would then walk together to our home in the Christian Quarter.

I honked the horn for the night staff to open the black, wrought-iron gate—and that's when *she* stepped through and walked past my old white Mercedes.

Oh my! Impulsively, I jumped out of the car. "Marie!" I shouted. "Marie! Marie!"

At the third shout, she looked back. Who was this crazy man, yelling her name while a nice lady sat calmly in his car? Then she recognized me as part of the staff in Christ Church. I myself had heard about her because she was a volunteer there, but we had never had an opportunity to talk.

As a gentleman, I offered her a ride home, and she accepted. I jumped, smiling, into my car and told my mother that she would have to walk the short distance to our house by herself because I had to drive the new volunteer to her manager's house, where she was staying. My mother walked home alone through the Christian Quarter, wondering why her son had abandoned her to give a ride to some strange volunteer!

I told Marie it was not a good idea for an American girl to walk alone in the dark from Jaffa Gate all the way to the Arnona neighborhood, a walk of at least thirty minutes. And I *knew*. I had just met my future wife. This was the woman I wanted to share my dreams and life with.

Of course I never told her so—she'd have thought I was crazy. But I felt the presence of the Holy Spirit so strongly that at one point I almost stopped the car. I dropped Marie off safely and returned rejoicing to the Old City. I explained to my mother what had happened. And that night I slept very well.

## An American Girl Comes to Israel

When my beloved wife, Marie Howanstine Moubarak, first came to Jerusalem, she knew nothing of Palestinian Arab Christians. She was raised in a small town in southern Maryland among quiet forests and farms on the western shore of Chesapeake Bay. The eldest child of an Episcopal pastor, she grew up in the rectory of the church where her father served. Her home in rural Calvert County was surrounded by graveyards, and her friends refused to play with her there because they thought the area was haunted. Not surprisingly, Marie had a vivid imagination and a heightened awareness of the spiritual realm, and she was fearful of many things.

But although Marie's upbringing was the opposite of mine, which was marked by the bustle and chaos of Jerusalem's cosmopolitan Old City, our childhoods had at least one thing in common.

From the time she was three years old, Marie was taking people on tour! She would ask the young adults attending her family's home Bible study if they would like to buy a ticket to see her room. No money ever changed hands, of course, but the tour part was real. Marie would show her "tourists" her toys, books, and other important items.

Later, during her family's vacations in Texas, Marie would take the lead, making an itinerary of all their favorite things to do and places to see. She loved to sit in the front seat with the map, helping her dad navigate and looking for good places to stop, and she kept a journal of each day.

Despite her fears in the post-9/11 world, God began to draw Marie to the Middle East even as He drew her closer to Himself. In January 2002, during the Second Intifada, she visited Israel with her father to see what was happening at the epicenter of the conflict in Jerusalem. She stayed at the Christ Church guesthouse for three days and nights, not knowing that her future husband was working there and living just a few blocks away.

Unimpressed by Israel, Marie returned to her daily life in the United States. But she struggled to relate to friends and coworkers who were woefully ignorant about the Middle East and its peoples. After nine months of listening to their rantings, Marie decided to obtain a degree in secondary education so she could teach world social studies to high school students. She wanted to raise teenagers' awareness of other cultures so they could become better citizens of the world.

Marie studied every world religion and culture and their regional histories, but none of them offered absolute truth or peace. Their conflicting philosophies had instead resulted in many wars over the centuries across the globe. Overwhelmed, Marie finally stepped away from the university for a season in order to hear God's voice and find healing for her soul. In a quiet seaside town in April 2005, she privately dedicated herself to following

Jesus without reserve, wherever and however He would lead her, and waited for His instructions about what to do next.

One month prior, Marie had a remarkable epiphany. In an audible voice, God told her that she was destined to take people on field trips that would change their lives. She held on to that promise, not knowing how much she would have to sacrifice in order to follow God's calling on her life.

The very same evening that Marie committed her life to Jesus more deeply, her parents received a phone call from a ministry in Israel. There was a need; could Marie's father recommend someone who might fill it?

Yes, he could. The position fit Marie beautifully! With uncanny swiftness, a door had opened for Marie—a door back to Jerusalem and her destiny.

### Love Blossoms in Jerusalem

A couple days after I drove Marie home, our paths crossed again at the Heritage Center Museum, where I worked. Marie was taking a break from her own job, wandering around drinking a cup of coffee. She was walking down the museum steps, admiring the reflections of her pretty-colored shoes off the polished stone, when I called her name. She was happy to see me! I asked her to join me for her coffee break and tell me her story.

That evening we had our first date in Ein Karem, the village where tradition holds that John the Baptist was born. At a nice restaurant in this attractive outer suburb of Jerusalem, I shared my own story with Marie, and we opened up to each other almost instantly. She told me about her weaknesses and that she was scared of demons. I enjoyed listening to her because I had grown up with a gift of releasing people from demons! Marie's weakness was my strength, and my weaknesses were her strengths.

We dated for the next several months, and every time we met, something great happened. The Holy Spirit was in everything we did. Pastors who saw us sitting together in the Christ Church courtyard would come and pray for our relationship, not knowing anything about us. It was as if the whole universe was working for Marie and me to be together, and rumors about us spread all over the Old City.

One day Marie contracted chickenpox. I cared so much about her that I bought her flowers and asked to see her. Then I drove to her Arnona neighborhood, took her to a nice garden, and gave her the flowers—and proposed to her. And sick and all, Marie said yes!

Those were the happiest moments of my life. Marie gradually recovered, and we decided to have a family engagement party. Marie's parents came all the way from the United States one week before the party.

We set our wedding date for January 6, 2007, the feast of Epiphany. We were married in the chapel of the Notre Dame Guest House, just outside the Old City. Our wedding was unique because we included everyone we were involved with, so several languages were spoken. Our Arabic priest, Abuna Rafiq, did a great job. My Christian community and friends attended, as did my Jewish and Muslim friends and people from all over the world. The liturgy of the prayers was in Aramaic, and on the Order of Service given to our guests, we translated the mass into English.

Quiet prevailed during the mass; the presence of the Holy Spirit was so strong that my mother-in-law decided to worship with the "Hallelujah" song, which embraces all languages and denominations. The atmosphere was so peaceful that you could not hear a single noise anywhere. Afterward, at the reception at Christ Church, all our families and friends—Christians, Jews, and Muslims—came together, talking and sharing our joy. The paths of Andre and Marie had united, and a love story without an end had begun.

■ ■ ■

Marie has been my Veronica. When I have felt exhausted and burdened by my responsibilities, she has wiped my face with her veil of compassion, comfort, and encouragement. With Marie I feel comfortable and safe sharing my feelings, fears, and sadness. When I am weak and vulnerable, Marie softly wipes away my tears, sees God's truth in my life, and lovingly encourages me to continue walking forward into my destiny.

Marie is a woman of tremendous character. It took courage for her to leave her town, her country, her friends, almost everyone she knew, and move to Israel. She has needed courage to behave like a human being in the face of the often inhuman treatment we have experienced outside our circle of friends and our community of faith, in a city where ideologies and cultures clash in ways that often are unfair and cruel. Marie did not join the crowd, and that takes courage—courage to go against the tide, to be singled out. She is one to whom the King will one day say, "Whatever you did for one of the least of these brothers and sisters of mine, you did for me" (Matt. 25:40 NIV).

———

*Lord, how much courage we need to proclaim aloud that we love You, we care for You, we believe in You! Yes, Lord, we need courage, because many a time we are afraid to be laughed at for our principles, for our faith.*

*Jesus, make me mature enough to be able to stand up for Your truth without fear or prejudice! Help me to be responsible for the things You have called me to do in this life, to have the courage to take new steps and make mature decisions without being afraid of other people or our surroundings, and to glorify Your name in all that I do.*

# CHAPTER 7

# Jesus Falls
# the Second Time

Images depicting the seventh station show Jesus collapsing under the weight of the cross. For a few minutes He had a respite thanks to Simon of Cyrene, but the Roman soldiers' motive for enlisting Simon was sheer practicality, a matter of letting Jesus regain enough strength to take the cross back up and carry it Himself. Compassion wasn't part of the equation for these men; they enjoyed making their prisoners suffer as much as possible, and they were good at it.

STATION VII

Jesus is depleted from dehydration, hunger, lack of sleep, pummeling by the soldiers, and loss of blood from being shredded by a Roman flagellum. And once again He is encumbered with the heavy lumber. His legs tremble under its weight. He feels the pain, the loneliness, the humiliation. He prays silently to the Father and tries to keep moving in order to avoid more lashes from the soldiers. The stones hurt His feet.

And now suddenly, once again He finds Himself face down on the ground with the crossbeam heavy on the back of His neck. He tries to get up. He cannot take more lashes; He cannot afford to weaken further in this last part of His battle.

## The Seventh Station

After leaving the sixth station, you continue up the steps to the top of the hill, passing a barber shop to the left and a large food and fruit store. The seventh station is situated at a busy T-junction where the Via Dolorosa meets Souq Khan el-Zeit (Oil Market) Street in the center of the Old City.

According to tradition, this station marks the place where Jesus passed through the Gate of Judgment on His way to the hill of Calvary. The intersection is one of the busiest in the Old City and may also have been so in Jesus's day.

Standing in front of station seven, looking down to the left you will see the fragment of a column, probably Byzantine, marking this station. The door before you opens into a small Franciscan chapel. Inside the chapel, an ornately framed picture above the altar shows Jesus falling under the weight of the cross, and beneath the altar, a wall painting depicts the same scene. Stairs by the entry lead up to a second level that is not open to the public. A childhood friend of mine once lived in a home right on top of this station, and many times, as kids, we would play with the archeological remains up there.

##  Seeing beyond Ourselves

Every Christian following in the footsteps of Jesus must pick up their cross and carry it as He did. Palestinian Christians in this city carry crosses unique to their lives in Jerusalem. Life in the Old City is very hard for our tiny Christian minority. This is partly because, in our individual struggles to survive in a hostile environment, we focus on ourselves. My prayer is that we believers in the Christian Quarter will learn how to give up ourselves for the sake of others, just as Jesus did before us.

Living like a real Christian is not easy. It requires obedience to God and self-sacrifice, and it may be harder in the Holy Land than in many other places on earth. It is particularly difficult in Jerusalem, where the majority of the population are Jews and Muslims and the prejudice and oppression are a real and daily experience. Many residents of the Christian Quarter have emigrated away, and they continue to do so.

Often I have been tempted to join them. It would be easy to

leave for America. Half my family on my mother's side live in California and Illinois, and my wife is fully American, with family spread out all over the United States. I could get a nice job and have an easy life without much suffering. But it would be like running away. I was born in the Old City of Jerusalem for a reason. God chose me to be a tour guide in my homeland and to be a witness for Christ to multitudes of visitors from all the nations of the world—and to my own community. Many of my neighbors and old school friends suffer from depression, alcoholism, and drug abuse. Some have even committed suicide.

So whatever happens, I will not leave this place where I belong. Jerusalem is a battle zone, and I am always on the front lines, carrying heavy responsibilities. But Jesus passed through *all* the stations of the cross, and we Palestinian Christians must likewise endure and be strong. We must be salt and light in the dark streets of the Old City of Jerusalem.

## Isaac and Ishmael

"Did you hear about the bomb attack in Zion Square last night?" my mother asked. "Thirteen people were killed and about one hundred injured."

Yes, I knew. In the prologue, you can read about how God supernaturally intervened to save my life during that horrible attack in December 2001. But not wanting to worry my mother, I pretended I knew nothing about it. I told no one in my family for six months. They would have been terrified, so I waited until the right moment.

That night of the bombings was one of the hardest experiences of my life. Images of scattered bodies, blood flying through the air, and windows exploding in front of me were blasted into my brain. For several years I suffered from flashbacks, and some nights I could not sleep at all. A year passed before I could walk on Ben

Yehuda Street again, and for a long time I took a different route to my bank near Zion Square.

I had almost been killed by a Muslim fanatic. *Why? Why did people kill themselves and others?* It made no sense to me. Nevertheless, the conflict in the Middle East, especially in Israel, is real, and its roots in religious ideology are ancient.

At its core are two biblical brothers, Ishmael and Isaac, both sons of Abraham. The Bible tells us that Abraham and Sarah, impatient to have children, tried to "assist" God's plan by having a child through Sarah's Egyptian servant, Hagar. The result was Ishmael, born of the flesh rather than according to God's promise (Gen. 16; Gal. 4:22–23). When God finally did fulfill His promise to Abraham and Sarah, they had a son whom they named Isaac. The two sons, Isaac and Ishmael, were rivals from the start (Gen. 16:11–12), and their descendants have remained so to this day.

This didn't happen in a vacuum. The original enmity between Sarah and Hagar culminated in Hagar and her son's expulsion from the family shortly after Isaac was weaned (Gen. 21:8–20). Ishmael, fourteen years older than Isaac, was by then a young man, old enough to fully feel the inhumanity of being banished with his mother into the desert.

No doubt Ishmael felt the lash of Sarah's resentment long before. He knew he was far from the favored son. But imagine being driven out of a lifestyle of plenty into a struggle for survival. Suddenly Ishmael found himself thrust out of the tents he had long called home, where meat and drink were plenty, into a daily search for water, food, and shelter.

Isaac was too young to have had a hand in the matter, yet no wonder Ishmael bore a grudge against his younger brother. The harsh, unfair treatment bred a bitter sibling rivalry that continues today between Isaac's descendants, the Israelis, and Ishmael's descendants, the Arab people. No human effort—no political

solution, no peace negotiations—can bring real, lasting peace to
the Middle East. I have seen firsthand why this is so.

##  Moderate Voices for Peace

Who would ever have thought it possible—six Muslims, seven
Jews, and three Christians engaging in deep, heartfelt reconciliation. Bitter enemies weeping, asking for forgiveness for the trage-
dies and injustices inflicted on one another. People connecting as
people, transcending their differences, feeling each other's pain,
fear, and sadness and, for the first time in their lives, truly understanding each other. It was wonderful!

The year was 2004, and I had been chosen to represent the
Christian community of Jerusalem in a prestigious program spon-
sored by the YMCA. The program was called MVP, Moderate
Voices for Peace, and I was one of sixteen young adults who were
selected from Israel's different ethnic and religious groups, trained
in constructive dialogue, and sent to the United States for a reconciliation retreat and speaking tour. I was privileged to represent
the Palestinian Christian position to senators in Washington and
even inside the White House, and to explain my identity to others
who had probably never met, or even heard of, an Arab Christian
from Jerusalem.

Our group took many classes on conflict resolution. Israeli and
Palestinian team members spent hours in conversation. It was so
real! Many of us were crying and sharing how our families had in
many cases lied to us. A religious Jew in the program came to the
Palestinians and said, "Forgive me. My family lied to me all my life.
They raised me to hate Arabs and put curses on them when I see
them in the streets. Today I hear a different story from you, and I
can understand your perspective too."

And several Palestinians said to the Jewish team members,
"Forgive us. We did not realize how hard your lives were, and we

never studied about the Holocaust. We were taught it was only a story fabricated by the Jews as an excuse to get the land."

We built strong foundations with one another. Peace truly seemed possible; at last, serious negotiations between Palestinians and Jews appeared within reach. We finished the program, went back to Israel, and commenced follow-up meetings at the YMCA in West Jerusalem.

Within a week of one of our meetings, another bomb attack took place. Twelve Jews were killed in Ben Yehuda Street, not far from our meeting place. In the subsequent meeting, the Israelis became stubborn and the Muslims even more stubborn. Everyone defended his own ethnic or religious group. It was as if all the time we had spent together counted for nothing. All the programs we had been through, all the things we had learned, had no value in real-life situations. Everyone took his own side.

I sat quietly in that meeting, until finally I mentioned that no one was ready to sacrifice as Jesus did on the cross. Rage had erupted in the room. The brothers Isaac and Ishmael were fighting again.

They all needed Jesus in their lives. They needed to see the love of God, the forgiveness of Jesus, and understand what He did on the cross for all of us. Only when both groups of my friends, the Jews and the Muslims, accept Jesus in their lives and are forgiven, saved, and healed from generations of hatred will they be able to forgive each other and live together peacefully. Then the real peace will take place in Jerusalem.

## ♡ The One Great Hope

Get a Jewish person to open up to you and you will hear about the Holocaust, how hard life has been, how the Arabs hate them, and how the rest of the world hates them as well. A Palestinian will recite a similar litany about how his people lost their homes in 1948 and became refugees. He will tell you about the injustices and humiliation they have experienced, and about how the world, especially the West, hates them.

The Israelis and Palestinians are just like Ishmael and Isaac. Both need to stop acting like children, blaming each other, and seeing themselves as victims. They need to move on, grow up, get healed, and look for a brighter future. Until this happens, I don't think peace can become real.

Yet I still hope for peace, and it may even be starting to happen. Many Jews are giving their lives to Christ. They are called Messianic Jews, and they have congregations and meetings all over Israel. There is also a big community of former Muslims who are now believers in Jesus as the Messiah, both in Israel and in the West Bank, and they too meet every week in different locations.

One of my best friends is a Jew who rides a tank in the Israeli army, but he is saved by the blood of Jesus. Another of my friends is a former Muslim who served for a time in the Palestinian Liberation Organization, but he too is now a follower of Jesus. When the three of us meet, you can see the joy and forgiveness in our eyes and feel the presence of the Holy Spirit all over our lives.

There is a solution and there is hope. It is through Jesus Christ.

Both Isaac and Ishmael need to be saved by the blood of Christ and be transformed by the Holy Spirit. God is using us Palestinian Christians—the minority—to bring hope, love, and reconciliation between the two brothers. God has placed us between them like a bridge that spans a vast divide.

■　■　■

Why did God allow me to experience something as horrible as the 2001 bomb attack? For a long time I sought God for insights about that nearly fatal experience. And in time I heard His answer: He would use me to bring love and reconciliation to the Muslims.

I forgave the terrorists who were involved and washed myself of all the blood that was shed that night, asking God to forgive the attackers. I felt so released, and God enabled me to see the event in a positive way. I could look ahead and be part of the solution, not part of the problem. I could seek to bring life to people. I could be a means for the Holy Spirit to enter their lives.

> One thing I do, forgetting those things which are behind and reaching forward to those things which are ahead, I press toward the goal for the prize of the upward call of God in Christ Jesus.                    (PHIL. 3:13–14)

All of us who follow in Jesus's footsteps will experience times when we stumble and fall in life, not just once or twice but many times as we carry our cross. We may fall because of something that is done to us by others, or because of something we bring upon ourselves, or because of circumstances that simply happen in life. The important thing is the attitude we choose when it happens.

Will we, like Isaac and Ishmael, grovel on the ground, brooding over our injuries and refusing to rise above them? Or will we, like Jesus, see something bigger than ourselves—a vision that compels us to get back up and press forward for the prize of human hearts?

---

*Dear Lord, so many times I have wondered why I have to fall and pick myself up again! Many times I have stumbled on my path and called upon You. You always helped me to stand back up! How I wish to hide in Your love whenever I feel the burden of my cross! How I wish to come out of the mud whenever I stumble. The knowledge of Your love for me comes back as I see You again under the weight of the cross. My sins have added their weight too. Dear Lord, at this station, I am not going to ask for anything but just thank You from my heart for the love You have for each one of us. I want to be one with You, Jesus, and I want to carry the burdens of my life with a smile, with hope, and with life. Thank You, Jesus!*

*My beautiful bride, Marie, and I on our wedding day. We're in the Tower of David Museum, which used to be Herod's Palace, inside Jaffa Gate.*

Me, sitting amid the ruins of
a Palestinian village destroyed
during the 1948 war.

My beloved wife and
life partner, Marie.

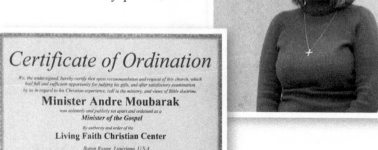

## Certificate of Ordination

We, the undersigned, hereby certify that upon recommendation and request of this church, which
had full and sufficient opportunity for judging his gifts, and after satisfactory examination
by us in regard to his Christian experience, call to the ministry, and views of Bible doctrine.

### Minister Andre Moubarak

was solemnly and publicly set apart and ordained as a
**Minister of the Gospel**

By authority and order of the Gospel

### Living Faith Christian Center

Baton Rouge, Louisiana, U.S.A.

On the 11th day of October 2015

Bishop Raymond W. Johnson, Pastor        Mildred F. Johnson, Vice President

My certificate of ordination.

With my dad, Yousef,
and mom, Reema,
on Palm Sunday.

**My twin brother Tony
and I as children.**

Mom holding us
outside our house
in the Old City.

Me on the right,
Tony on the left.
We look so alike!

Aerial photo showing locations of the stations of the cross.

"Via Dolorosa" in three languages. From top to bottom: Hebrew, Arabic, and English.

*Walking the Via Dolorosa with a group from South Africa.*

*The street that leads to my old house in the Christian Quarter.*

*Early morning and a rare sight: the Via Dolorosa empty.*

*One of many views inside the Church of the Holy Sepulcher.*

*Christian nuns.*

**Three great world religions meet in the Via Dolorosa.**

*Muslim boy.*

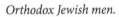

*Orthodox Jewish men.*

# PART 2

# Stations Eight
# through Fourteen

# CHAPTER 8

# Jesus Meets the Women of Jerusalem

Have you ever heard it said that "the Jews killed Jesus"? That misconception, propagated throughout Christendom, lies at the root of centuries of anti-Semitism. But you don't have to read between the lines of Scripture to see that it's not true—you just have to let the lines speak for themselves. At the eighth station of the cross, we have an opportunity to let the Scriptures paint a different, more accurate picture as Jesus encounters the women of Jerusalem.

STATION

**VIII**

Luke 23:27 tells us that "a great multitude of the people followed Him, and women who also mourned and lamented Him." These were not jeering crowds, as is commonly imagined, but grieving crowds. Most Jewish people were heartbroken, not glad, when Jesus was crucified. A mere handful of powerful leaders from Jerusalem engineered Jesus's death, and they had to proceed with great care because of His popularity (Matt. 21:45–46). Moreover, only Pontius Pilate—a Roman, not a Jew—had the authority to order His execution.

But let's not miss the real point. Jesus did not die as a helpless victim of either Jewish or Roman injustice. He *chose* to die on the cross in faithfulness to the Father's will in order to bear the sin of the world.

Who really crucified Jesus? You and I. It was *our* sins that nailed Him to the cross. The eighth station of the cross calls us to turn from accusing others and consider instead our own guilt, to recognize our need to be cleansed by the blood of the Lamb of God, and to walk righteously.

The eighth station is my favorite station. It is nearest to my parents' house, and I grew up on these roads. I played for hours here. I jumped on every step, touched every corner, and have memories of every single stone in this area.

Let us imagine how it was here two thousand years ago. The crowd following the procession has grown. The women gather in the streets, and Jesus hears them weeping and crying out for Him. Such sights and sounds were common when disaster struck or a loved one died, just as they are common today. Jesus had heard similar wailing at Jairus's house in Capernaum and in Bethany when Lazarus died (Mark 5:38–40; John 11:31–33). Now the lamentation is for Him.

He turns to the grieving women, compassion mingled with pain in His voice. "Daughters of Jerusalem," He tells them, "do not weep for me, but weep for yourselves and for your children" (Luke 23:28).

Strange, unsettling words from a man on His way to be executed! As we shall see, there is more to them than lies at the surface.

# ✖ The Eighth Station

Turning away from Souq Khan el-Zeit Street, you walk sixteen steps up an alley called Al-Khanaqah Street. Station eight is marked by a stone on the left, bearing a sign with the Greek inscription "IC-XC NI-KA." It means "Jesus Christ Victorious."

The sign was dedicated by the Greek Orthodox Church of St. Charalampos, whose monastery is behind the wall. A humble, peaceful man from the shop will offer to sell you a pamphlet about the Via Dolorosa for a dollar. I highly recommend this purchase because it has Bible verses and a short explanation about each station of the Via Dolorosa.

Continuing up the stairs and turning right at the first stairway, you will pass a bakery and an Ethiopian convent. At the end of this street, you will find my old home where I grew up. Walking through here at 8:00 a.m., you can smell the fresh Arab bread called *kaeek*, which I eat for breakfast almost every day.

The streets of my old neighborhood are very dirty. This is not what residents here want; it is just how things are. But I have great hope that better days are coming. For now, let us turn from the blight of these streets to the sorrow and the drama of the eighth station of the cross.

## ♡ The Dry Wood of Hate

> A great multitude of the people followed Him, and women who also mourned and lamented Him. Jesus, turning to them, said, "Daughters of Jerusalem, do not weep for Me, but weep for yourselves and for your children." (LUKE 23:27–28)

*What?* the women must have thought. *He is the one suffering and dying, yet He is telling us to grieve for our own sakes. Why?*

Jesus knew what was in store for Jerusalem. His language here foreshadows the horrors that would engulf the city four decades later. The Hebrew word for "daughters" is *banot*, and when used next to a person's name, it means female children. But when used next to a place, the word has a broader, metaphorical meaning.

The expressions "daughter of Israel," "daughters of Jerusalem," and "daughters of my people" all refer to the poor, the multitudes, the ordinary people.

The Hebrew word for "city" is feminine. The city's protective wall is its skirt, so to speak, and those living in suburbs outside the wall are its daughters. Jesus's words here to the "daughters of

Jerusalem" reflect his concern for these people in the future. They will be killed first when the Romans come to destroy Jerusalem in AD 70. Jesus continues:

> "For indeed the days are coming in which they will say, 'Blessed are the barren, wombs that never bore, and breasts which never nursed!' Then they will begin 'to say to the mountains, "Fall on us!" and to the hills, "Cover us!"' For if they do these things in the green wood, what will be done in the dry?" (LUKE 23:29–31)

Even in His own suffering, Jesus looks prophetically to another human tragedy. If they do this when the wood is green, He says, what will they do when it is dry? By "they," He is most likely referring to the Romans. If they can crucify the "green wood" of Jesus—whose message was of grace, forgiveness, and tolerance and in whom Pilate acknowledged he could find no fault—then what would they do in coming years to the "dry wood" of a rebellious Judea whose political and religious leaders incited violence both against the Romans and against fellow Jews who held different views?

Consider the symbolism of the dry wood. The Zealots, a Jewish political sect who advocated the violent overthrow of Roman power, spearheaded the disastrous First Jewish-Roman War (AD 66–73). The Romans had a name for the Zealots: firebrands. It described their practice of throwing torches of dry wood wrapped with cloth and dipped in olive oil at Roman troops. These crude but deadly incendiary devices typified the "dry wood" not only of the Jews' violent hatred of Rome but also of one another. After the Second Temple was destroyed in AD 70, rabbis who reconvened the Sanhedrin in Yavneh claimed that the Jewish War had been lost not because of Roman military superiority but because of causeless internal hatred. The war was not just Jew against Roman; it was also Jew against Jew.

If to overcome hate, you yourself also hate, then the only victor is hatred. You have to be big enough to say, "Father, forgive them, for they do not know what they are doing." You have to be strong enough to stop the spiral of violence.

The Zealots killed Romans, and so the Romans arrested Zealots; today, Palestinians try to kill Jews, and Jews arrest Palestinians. The Zealots abducted Romans to trade for imprisoned Zealot leaders; today, Palestinians do much the same thing. We live in a time when few Palestinian and Jewish leaders are saying that we have to respect our enemy enough to talk to him.

Love your enemy. If you have enough respect for your enemy, you will realize they have difficulties as well. This is Jesus's message for all times.

##  Hope for the Christian Quarter

Down came the rain—hard. And that was fine with me. I liked watching the rain.

I was a boy playing on the steps here by the eighth station, and when I felt the first fat drops, I sought shelter under a rusty awning opposite the Charalampos monastery. Heavier and heavier grew the downpour, and the water started to flood the streets. All the cats began running for cover—I could hear their cries.

The rain continued, and the storm drain began to flood. And now rats and mice began to emerge from the underground sewer pipes, along with all kinds of rubbish and junk from the Christian Quarter. Ugly things that had long been hidden were coming to the surface in the rain.

The rain cleanses everything. And that is how the Holy Spirit operates in our lives. He brings to the surface things that are not pretty to look at, hidden sins and wounds, in order to cleanse and heal us. We so need Him to be present in our daily walk with Christ!

Jesus's words to the daughters of Jerusalem long ago speak to the Christian Quarter today: "Don't worry about Me; look at yourselves, how you live in sin and darkness. Do not grieve for Me; grieve for yourselves." Grieve for the drug abuse, the depression, the poverty, the spirit of suicide. Grieve for hearts devoid of hope, ambition, and meaning. Grieve for how the devil has destroyed families and lives.

My own life changed after I met Jesus. How blessed I am to have been delivered from my filth and sin! I have been washed from all the unforgiveness, hatred, darkness, and hard life of the Christian Quarter. Jesus has transformed me and made me salt and light in my community. He has given me the joy of the Holy Spirit and success in my life—and now I want these same things for all my friends and neighbors. I want their world to become better. I want their streets to become cleaner. I want them to live their lives far from the lies of the enemy. There are so many young kids here with talents, ambitions, and dreams to be fulfilled and directed by the Spirit of God. How I long for their hearts to be opened to Jesus!

So I pray for my community in the Old City. I pray that the Holy Spirit will cleanse the Christian Quarter, washing this neighborhood and making its streets clean and bright.

I believe I see this starting to happen. Many Christian friends are doing good works here, trying clean up the Christian Quarter. These local believers want to bring a better lifestyle into the Quarter and have a positive impact on the community. Even since I began writing this book, hope has been increasing in these streets. Like the rain that washes and waters the earth, the Holy Spirit is moving through His people, bringing cleansing, hope, life, and growth.

If anyone is to blame for the death of Jesus, it is you and I.

> All we like sheep have gone astray;
> We have turned, every one, to his own way;
> And the Lord has laid on Him the iniquity of us all.
>
> (ISA. 53:6)

Here at station eight, we can join the women of Jerusalem in weeping not only for Jesus but also for ourselves. In His death we see what we deserve, we rightly feel appalled, and the mystery of grace astounds us. "For [God] made Him who knew no sin [Jesus] to be sin for us, that we might become the righteousness of God in Him" (2 Cor. 5:21).

Jesus has borne our sin so that we might be forgiven. He died in our place so that we might live in His place forever.

---

*Dear Lord, help me not to blame others for the death of Jesus but to see my own sin as sending Him to the cross. To whatever extent anti-Semitism dwells in me and other Christians, please forgive us and cleanse our minds and hearts. Help us to grasp the mystery of Your grace and act on it by searching ourselves for bigotry of any kind against any people group—for Your heart and kingdom extends to all nations, tongues, and tribes. Let us see in the death of Jesus that which gives us all life and love, not more death and hatred. May our distress over the suffering of Jesus and our sorrow over our own sin turn to joy when we recognize the majesty of Your mercy.*

# CHAPTER 9

# Jesus Falls
# the Third Time

It is not much farther now to the hilltop on which Jesus will be crucified. But the rugged crossbeam He carries is so heavy, and Jesus's strength is almost depleted. He is thirsty, very thirsty, and His mind is foggy from dehydration and loss of blood. His foot catches on a stone, and He staggers forward, fights momentarily for balance, loses the battle, and down He goes yet a third time, the piece of lumber clattering to the ground beside Him.

STATION

IX

A man may fall many times on his way to fulfilling his God-given destiny. For Jesus, this is the last time. The question is, can He get up again?

> The steps of a good man are ordered by the LORD, and He delights in his way. Though he fall, he shall not be utterly cast down; for the LORD upholds him with his hand. (PS. 37:23–24)

Jesus arises, swaying unsteadily at first but with a look of fierce resolve in His eyes. Nothing will stop Him from completing the short, final leg of His journey to the place where His mission will be fulfilled.

Two of the soldiers pick up the beam from both ends and hoist it back up onto His shoulders, and once again Jesus steps forward.

## The Ninth Station

**Let's go back to Souq Khan el-Zeit Street and turn right on this busy Turkish Ottoman–style market road.** We pass a local Arab coffee roaster and smell the strong, rich brew on the breeze. Further up the hill, our route across Souq Khan el-Zeit leads to a pastry shop called Zalatymo, whose specialty is *mutabak*, an oven-baked sweet filled with cheese and walnut. For a few shekels the owner will take you inside and show you a segment of the second-century Roman Cardo which remains intact inside his shop.

**From here, walk up twenty-eight stone steps and you will come to the ninth station marked by a cross on a pillar. The green door on the left leads to the yard of the Ethiopian Quarter.**

## Six-Way Division

In 1853 the Church of the Holy Sepulcher was divided into six territorial areas between three major denominations: Greek Orthodox, Roman Catholic, and Armenian; and three minor denominations: Coptic, Assyrian, and Ethiopian. The building's chaotic history is evident in its mixture of styles—Byzantine, medieval, Crusader, and modern—as each Christian community has decorated its particular space and shrines in its own distinctive way. A set of complicated rules governs the transit of groups from other denominations across each section on any given day, and some boundaries remain disputed.

Among the six denominations that occupy the Church of the Holy Sepulcher, the Ethiopian church is the poorest. It has no actual property in the Holy Sepulcher, only access rights. Its monks live on the roof of the church. Their modest huts have not been repaired due to conflict with their neighbors, the Egyptian Copts.

The entrance to the Ethiopian monks' compound and their small monastery, Deir es-Sultan, also called St. Michael's Church, is up some stairs from the ninth station through the green door mentioned earlier. It is said that in the wake of the Queen of Sheba's visit to King Solomon, a son was born. He came to Jerusalem as an adult and later returned to his homeland, taking with him the ark of the covenant, which some believe is kept in Aksum, Ethiopia, to this very day.

Near the ninth station, on your right side opposite the Ethiopian Quarter, is the small Coptic Orthodox Church of St. Helena. If you go inside, ask the priest who is sitting there to show you the entrance to the large underground cistern. He will point toward a small door, beyond which lies a long dark tunnel. Once inside, you can't see more than two feet in front of you! But the tunnel will take you to a huge, open lake. The acoustics are amazing! It's cool that something so immense is hidden in the Old City, unknown to a lot of people. This large cistern was discovered by Queen Helena and once provided water to the Sepulcher.

Upon leaving the Coptic Church, you will walk through a big green door and, a few steps farther, find yourself on the rooftop courtyard of the Holy Sepulcher Church. Several other interesting sites are close by. The cupola on the left is the top of the underground Armenian Chapel of St. Helena. On the right side of the courtyard is the entrance to the Ethiopian Church of St. Michael, mentioned above. It is entered by a staircase from the courtyard. Be careful—you have to bend down because of the low doorframe; I warn tourists of this every time, but they still bump their heads! On the right-hand wall is a painting of King Solomon receiving the Queen of Sheba (1 Kings 10:1). Enter this church and continue all the way down the steps until you reach the front courtyard of the Holy Sepulcher.

## Where Is the Love?

You will have noticed that we passed from Coptic territory to Ethiopian territory. Much of the conflict in Jerusalem is about territory, and it doesn't just take place on a large scale. On July 30, 2002, here at the Church of the Holy Sepulcher, mounting tension between Ethiopian and Coptic priests, monks, and nuns broke out into a fierce fistfight as the priests accused each other of violating the sensitive Status Quo agreement governing the division of the roof between them. As black-clad monks threw stones and iron bars at each other, the Israeli police were called to restore order. Eleven monks had to be treated at a nearby hospital.

This particular dispute goes back to a nineteenth-century epidemic that killed most of the Ethiopians who controlled the entire roof at that time. This enabled the Egyptian Copts to take over. A deal worked out the previous century, in 1757 under Sultan Osman III, had given each denomination control over specific parts of the church, and violations—whether accidental or deliberate, and sometimes over such petty matters as who cleans where inside the ancient chambers—can result in violent flare-ups. In the 1920s, the British Mandatory authority resurrected the 1757 division, giving the roof and its buildings back to the Ethiopians, but the Copts were allowed to retain the small monastery on the roof. The incident in 2002 was not the first time monks had come to blows in Christendom's most holy place, but it was one of the most serious in recent years.

Religious conflicts between Christians over territory don't take place only in Jerusalem. A similar fight broke out in Bethlehem's Church of the Nativity on December 28, 2013, when dozens of monks from rival denominations who were cleaning the church brawled over territory with their brooms.

The Holy Sepulcher Church, known in the Eastern Orthodox tradition as the Anastasis Church or Church of the Resurrection, is one of the most complicated archeological and historical churches in the world. The emperor Constantine, who reigned from AD 306 to 337 and made Christianity the official religion of the Eastern Roman Empire, directed his mother, Queen Helena, to build churches on sites that commemorated the life of Jesus. The Church of the Holy Sepulcher was inaugurated in AD 325, and Helena was present in 326 at its construction. It was dedicated in

335. Previously, a second-century temple of Aphrodite had occupied the site, and the temple in turn may have once been erected over an earlier Christian shrine.

This fourth-century church was four times the size of today's Holy Sepulcher. It was damaged or destroyed by successive conquests and earthquakes and rebuilt by the Crusaders in the mid-twelfth century, using pillars from the original church. That rebuilt church, much smaller than the original, is essentially the church we see today.

The Holy Sepulcher Church, the traditional site of Jesus Christ's crucifixion and resurrection, has long been a tremendously sensitive source of disputes among the denominations. A prime example is the debate that began in the thirteenth century about who has the right to use the key to open the gates of the Holy Sepulcher each morning. The Greek Orthodox monks claimed this right on the grounds that they were the most ancient church in the city, with the earliest tradition. But the Roman Catholics said it was their right as the inheritors of the Crusaders, who came and fought for this land in the eleventh century and freed Jerusalem.

The dispute continued until a solution was reached to give the keys to one man from the Joudeh family and another man from the Nuseibeh family, two Jerusalem Palestinian clans who have been the custodians of the entrance to the Holy Sepulcher since the twelfth century.

One of the men comes in the morning, opens the doors of the church, and then sits on his famous chair to the left of the entrance. He also locks the door in the evening. The man from the other clan repeats that procedure the next day. This alternating arrangement works well.

■   ■   ■

The divisiveness and petty squabbling between denominations is no small thing. It is heartbreaking. Jesus prayed that we would be one as He and the Father are one (John 17:11, 20–23). Why are we not? It is pointless to talk about bringing reconciliation between Jews and Arabs when we Christians are so divided over trifling, worldly matters.

We have got to get our priorities straight. We may never agree on all points of doctrine or liturgy until Jesus comes, but we can unite in our love of Him and one another. He is our Cornerstone— the Person and Spirit of our Lord, not our teachings, our histories, our liturgies, or our traditions. When we prize temporal things more than eternal human hearts, we devalue what Jesus Himself values most. He laid down His very life for us, and we ought to have that same attitude toward one another (1 John 3:16). We must focus not on the things that divide us but on treating our brothers and sisters with generosity, kindness, and care. Only then can we have any credibility talking to Arabs and Jews about reconciliation.

##  Hope beyond Reason

Exhausted and wordless, Jesus has almost reached His destination, sometimes pushed along and sometimes dragged by the Roman soldiers, who carry the tools for crucifixion. He can hear the terrible screams of the other two prisoners who left the fortress with Him as the Romans crucify them. Some of the soldiers forcibly keep the people at bay. Others guard the steep northern side of Calvary's rocky outcrop lest anyone should fall. The Jewish guards, members of the Sanhedrin, and Jewish elders are also present.

One last time Jesus stumbles and falls. The soldiers and Jewish officials laugh at Him and mock Him. What runs through Jesus's mind as he lies there, straining to rise one more time in these final moments before the actual brutal act of crucifixion begins? Perhaps He recalls the words of David:

> The LORD is my light and my salvation;
> Whom shall I fear?

The LORD is the strength of my life;
Of whom shall I be afraid?
When the wicked came against me
To eat up my flesh,
My enemies and foes,
They stumbled and fell.
Though an army may encamp against me,
My heart shall not fear;
Though war may rise against me,
In this I will be confident.

One thing I have desired of the LORD,
That will I seek:
That I may dwell in the house of the LORD
All the days of my life,
To behold the beauty of the LORD,
And to inquire in His temple.

(PS. 27:1–4)

Humanly speaking, this is it for Jesus—the end of the road. Who cares that He has fallen again and perhaps injured Himself. The pain is about to get far worse. There is only One to whom He can turn now. One who keeps Jesus's spirit in the face of His deadly enemies, in the face of death itself. One to whose will Jesus has committed His entire life on earth.

His Father will bear Him up. His Father gives Him a hope and a promise beyond mortal reason, beyond what eyes can see.

Jesus rises again, steadies Himself, and carries his cross the last few yards to His destination: Golgotha, the Place of the Skull.

##  Falling on the Stones of Hatred

Amazingly, my windshield didn't shatter from the impact of the laptop-size rock the woman threw at it. But the crowd of enraged Jewish settlers swarming around my car near the West Bank town of Nablus[6] were only getting started. My vehicle might survive their violence, but would I?

It was an October day in 2008, and I was driving home after having my car fixed at a car repair shop in the West Bank. When my old Mercedes has mechanical issues, I usually take it to that particular place because they do a great job and I have a good relationship with the mechanic. There had been protests in the area of the settlements in Nablus, but I did not realize the area I was driving through was as dangerous as it turned out to be. Bad news on both sides is such a common, daily occurrence in West Bank that you get used to it and don't much care.

It took the mechanic two hours to fix my car. "Be careful driving home," he cautioned me. "The settlers have closed all the roads entering Jerusalem." But even he did not know how serious things were.

I hoped to get home and rest a bit before my shift at Christ Church Guest House started at 3:00 p.m. inside Jaffa Gate. But about twenty minutes into my normal route, traffic became congested, and many cars were turning back. "What's going on?" I asked a driver. Settlers were attacking Palestinian cars, came the reply. I was invited to follow some of the cars as they tried an alternate route to bypass the trouble. Another twenty minutes brought us to a side road just off the Huwara checkpoint south of Nablus. This straight and long road leads to Taybeh, a small Christian village, and then to Jerusalem. After thirty more minutes of high-speed driving, the road ahead looked empty and safe.

Then I noticed a minor checkpoint with several cars, maybe six, passing through it very s-l-o-w-l-y. As I drew close, I realized it was a settler-created checkpoint. If you were a Jewish driver, they would let you pass. As for a Palestinian like me, I didn't know what to expect.

Suddenly the driver in the car ahead of me hit the gas pedal and ran his car through the checkpoint. That was probably a clue, and now I was next. A settler came to my driver's-side window. He looked very upset, but I was not scared—yet—and anyway, showing fear would only make the situation worse.

I spoke with the man in Hebrew, but from my accent he knew I was an Arab. Suddenly his family and perhaps fifty other settlers surrounded my car. The father of the family, their mother, and other adults as well as young boys and girls all held huge rocks. And suddenly I grasped my situation: I was surrounded by fanatical religious Jewish settlers full of rage. They wanted to block every entrance to Jerusalem and take revenge on Arabs for what had happened two days before in Nablus, when Palestinian terrorists had shot two settlers in their cars.

The settlers started to throw stones at my car. My Mercedes is a strong car, but the situation was escalating seriously. Then I saw the father coming toward me and reaching for a gun at his side. I met his eye and saw the hatred inside him, but my own eyes showed love, even for my enemies, in this moment of my imminent death. My only recourse was to pray—there was no other option. So I prayed: "Jesus, my Lord, Holy Spirit, save me!"

The moment I finished my sentence, out of nowhere an Israeli police car raced up and slammed to a stop in front of me, scattering the settlers. I was seconds away from being shot; had not the police shown up at exactly that moment, I would have been dead. I was terrified, and as soon as I was able, I stomped on the gas and roared away toward Jerusalem.

Inside me a dilemma raged. Despite the love I tried to show the settlers, my flesh took control as I fled the checkpoint. I screamed a profanity; I wanted to curse those settlers for trying to kill me. Like Jesus, I had fallen on hard stones, stones of human hatred. Now would I, like Him, get up?

After maybe two minutes, suddenly I remembered Jesus on the cross. I prayed, "Lord, forgive them, because they do not know what they are doing." I felt as Jesus Himself might have felt. "If Jesus forgave, I will forgive," I told myself. "Despite all their bad actions, I love them. I am safe, I am alive, and I will bless them."

A tangible, strong presence of the Holy Spirit permeated the car. It was like a cloud covering me with peace and healing me from all I had just passed through. The time was almost 2:30, and I still had to pass through the main checkpoint to Jerusalem. But the crisis was over; now my only concern was not to arrive late for work.

For the second time in my life, I had been near death. The first time came through a fanatical Palestinian. I only just survived the bomb attack in 2001 because the Holy Spirit saved me. Now I had barely escaped being shot at point-blank range by an equally fanatical Jewish settler. The Holy Spirit had saved me again. These incidents caused me to become a strong friend of the Holy Spirit. I decided to get to know Him better and make Him my best friend in life. I never wanted to leave Him.

At work I changed shifts with my Jewish friend, who wondered why I was twenty minutes late. This man lives in a West Bank settlement near Jerusalem. It was hard for me to share with him what had happened; I was still in the moment, still visualizing how close I had come to death. I was nearly crying. My friend, a true Messianic Jew, saw how real the trauma was for me. He asked forgiveness on behalf of his people, and he hugged me—and that was real reconciliation from the heart.

Peace can come to Israel only if people get saved by the blood of Christ. This is the only way any of us can have the power to forgive our enemy truly and from our heart.

———

*Dear Jesus, I am wondering about all those with whom You shared Your life during Your ministry. I wonder why Peter denied You, why Judas betrayed You, why all the others left You except for John.*

*Why did Peter have to hear the cock's crow to realize he was mistaken? Was it not enough to hear Your warning? But while Judas turned away, Peter repented.*

*Yes, Lord, looking at Your disciples, I realize how weak I am and how many times I have left You too. Sometimes, like Peter, I did so just to protect my reputation in the world. At other times I even betrayed Your love, sinning and pursuing the world rather than You. Yet through it all, Lord, You carried me on Your shoulders and helped me rise again. Please fill my heart with strength so that whenever I feel like I'm about to fall, I will remember that You want me to walk upright in Your path.*

# CHAPTER 10

# Jesus Is Stripped
# of His Garments

Journey's end. Jesus is here at last. Here at Golgotha, the Place of the Skull, whose very name evokes the brutalities so frequently enacted on this hilltop. The soldiers pull away the crossbeam from Jesus's shoulders and throw it on the ground, and He stands, exhausted, waiting for what comes next. The watching crowd clamors round. Glancing up, Jesus sees the two thieves already hoisted in place on upright poles, one on either side of where He will be. They are screaming in pain. He shifts his gaze back down and awaits His turn.

STATION

X

The soldiers seize Jesus, laughing loudly. They strip off His clothes and throw them in a small heap. "You're not going to need these anymore," one soldier sneers.

"They're a mess," another soldier says to the others, "but wash them up and they'll be worth having."

"I want that seamless cloak."

"Share and share alike. That's a fine bit of cloth; tear it up and let's all have some."

"No, it's too nice for that. Leave it in one piece. Let's get Him up there with the others, and then we'll toss for it."

The soldiers, when they had crucified Jesus, took His garments and made four parts, to each soldier a part, and also the tunic. Now the tunic was without seam, woven from the top in one piece. They said therefore among themselves, "Let us not tear it, but cast lots for it, whose it shall be," that the Scripture might be fulfilled which says:

> "They divided My garments among them,
> And for My clothing they cast lots."          (JOHN 19:23–24)

Jesus stands in naked silence, His battered body now utterly exposed for all Jerusalem to see. Even the most fundamental aspect of human dignity, His modesty, has been taken from Him. Nothing of this earth remains in His possession anymore except one thing, the most precious of all. And He is about to lay that down as well, freely.

## ✖ The Tenth Station

If you picked up a cross at the first station to carry over the course of the Via Dolorosa, now you must return it before you proceed to station ten. Lean it back against the wall under the round roman numeral IX, and then cross the courtyard on your left. Go through the small green door at the end of it and head down through the Ethiopian chapel alongside the Church of the Holy Sepulcher, and then into the courtyard of the church itself (described in chapter 9).

Standing at the main entrance of the Holy Sepulcher Church, if you look up, you will see a three-arched stained-glass window. Below it is a wooden ladder made of cedar wood, possibly from Lebanon. It was first mentioned in 1757 and has remained in the same exact location since the eighteenth century, when an

agreement of Status Quo proposed by the Ottoman Sultan Osman III in February 8, 1852, defined the rights of the Greek Orthodox and Armenian Christian religious orders in the Holy Land, and particularly in the Church of the Holy Sepulcher. The Status Quo determines the subjects of ownership of the holy places, and more specifically, the spaces inside the sanctuaries. It also extends to the times and durations of functions, movements, the routes taken by the priests, and how different functions are implemented, whether by singing or by reading.

Both orders originally claimed the ladder as their property. But an Armenian monk who used the ladder to clean the window left it there, and it was standing in that spot when the sultan imposed the

Status Quo on both orders. All objects were frozen exactly where they were, including the ladder. Since the window belongs to the Armenian Church, and the basement where the ladder stands belongs to the Greek Orthodox church, the ladder caused a conflict. No solution has ever been found, so there the ladder remains.

Looking down the ladder, to the left you will see the main entrance to the Holy Sepulcher. Even today the rigid code of the Status Quo defines exactly when and how the main door of the basilica must be opened and closed. The keys are kept by two Muslim families, the Joudehs and the Nuseibehs, mentioned in the last chapter. Oddly, the door is locked from the outside!

The opening of the basilica is a ceremony in itself—a clue to the difficulties the Status Quo imposes on the denominations living within the precinct of the Holy Sepulcher. Prior to 1831, the opening and closing of the door was carried out by the two families only after the payment of a tax, which was abolished by Ibrahim Pasha in 1831.

Even the way the drainage system is run or new toilets are installed can create conflicts. These and other minor details have been disputed between the six Christian religious orders—the Latins (Roman Catholics), Greek Orthodox, Armenian, Syriac Orthodox, Coptic Christians, and Ethiopians.

**Enter the massive Church of the Holy Sepulcher through large, old wooden doors, and walk up the stairs to Calvary on your right. The tenth station, "Jesus is stripped of His garments," is in this area of the church in the Chapel of the Franks.**

The remaining four stations, eleven through fourteen, are all located inside the Holy Sepulcher near to the tenth station. They are as follows:

11. Crucifixion: Jesus is nailed to the cross (Roman Catholic side altar).

12. Jesus dies on the cross (main Greek Orthodox altar).

13. Jesus's body is removed from the cross and placed on the Anointing Stone (to the left of the main altar and down the steps).

14. Jesus is placed in the tomb (rotunda next to the big room near the Anointing Stone).

##  Dehumanized by Authority

*"Aatzor, aatzor!"* the three Israeli soldiers shouted at my friend and me. "Stop, stop!"

We stopped.

It was 10:30 on a beautiful summer night with a pleasant breeze, and we were walking back home through New Gate with some books we had purchased at a book fair at Kikar Safra (Safra Square) on Jaffa Road. I love books and had bought two written in English, one on the history of the Holy Land and another on the archaeology of the City of David, the area just below the Temple Mount, excavated in recent years.

We had passed my old school and descended the steps of the Apostles Road just before the Casa Nova guesthouse when the soldiers detained us. One, a young man of perhaps nineteen, slapped me on my chest and tried to strip off the front of my shirt with his hand.

*Why? What on earth had I done?*

"To the wall, to the wall! Put your faces to the wall," ordered another soldier. We complied.

"Hands up fast and spread your legs!" shouted the third. With his huge boot, he kicked me hard on my left leg so that my legs were stretched far apart. I could hardly stand while holding up my hands.

"Where did you come from?"

"From Jaffa Road bookstore," I replied.

"Where are you going?"

"To our houses in the Christian Quarter."

"So you live here?"

"Yes sir."

"Do you know what just happened?"

"What?" I asked.

One of the soldiers replied in Hebrew, "Ten minutes ago, a Palestinian stabbed a soldier in the Old City."

This was serious. For twenty minutes my friend and I endured hostility and mockery by the soldiers. Finally, after some muffled instruction on their walkie-talkies, they told us to go home.

The Bible tells how the Roman soldiers mocked Jesus on these same roads. Yet Jesus's response was to love them and pray for them. As a Jew, He had lived under the occupation of the Roman government, and His childhood had been that of a refugee, traveling with His parents from Bethlehem, where they had journeyed from Nazareth for the Roman census, to Egypt, where they fled with their child to protect His life, and then finally, when the danger has passed, back to Nazareth. Jesus certainly knew military oppression. Yet He never said any bad thing about any Roman soldier, ever, even though the Romans were His enemies.

### "Teudat Zehut"

Checkpoints are frequently hard on me because of my Arab ethnicity. Even entering Damascus Gate I have problems with the soldiers. I have never entangled myself in politics nor ever done anything illegal, yet I'm often stopped and asked for my ID.

One Friday, walking to work through the crowded market of the Christian Quarter, I found myself looking at people's faces and the ways they dressed. There were probably more than ten thousand Arabs there, mostly Muslims. I thought, *Why does everyone look so different?* Some have bigger eyes than others. Some have large, rugged hands, and others have small, delicate hands. And other features—all so different from each other. Not a single person looks exactly like another. Even my twin brother and I are different, even though we are "identical" twins.

The voice of an Israeli policeman jolted me from my thoughts: *"Atah, atah, boina,"* meaning, "You, you, come here." I went over. *"Teudat zehut"* ("Show me your ID").

The policeman too bore the stamp of uniqueness. Instead of reaching for my ID, I said to him, "I want to ask you a serious question." It was an unusual request, and it took him off guard.

"Quick," he said, humoring me.

"Why did you choose me out of all this crowd? There are thousands of human beings here and everyone is different from everyone else. Why me? I look like an angel among all those people. Why me?"

The soldier laughed at me and gestured with his hands that he thought I was crazy. But when I did not react as he continued to mock me, he finally motioned me on. "Just go," he said, not requesting my ID again.

I was still musing about uniqueness as I passed through Damascus Gate. The crowds there are thick, especially on Friday after prayers have finished at the mosques. At the top of the steps near the taxi station, I had a bird's-eye view all the way to the gate with its masses of people—all colors and kinds of clothes, faces of every age, people of all heights and body types mingling and jostling about. Such a milling, colorful tide of humanity! And that is when God spoke to my heart: "I love the world and I love all people, and so I have created them in all the different shapes and features that are possible. No one is the same as another."

I was surprised to have an answer, and one that satisfied me so well. I felt love for all these people, knowing that Jesus Christ indeed came and sacrificed Himself for each one of them, for the entire world.

■  ■  ■

Both of these experiences had humiliation as their common denominator. But humiliation is not the same thing as humility. A person can respond in different ways to degrading treatment. Humility is the response Jesus chose, and it is the one I want to walk in as well. When Jesus's last shred of dignity and personhood was stripped from Him before the crowd on the hilltop, He submitted in silence to the will of the Father. May the Lord grant you and me the grace to live our lives in that same humble spirit—for it is through the humble in heart that God displays the power of His kingdom.

## ♡ When Glory Is Stripped Away

In Jerusalem, the way you dress says a lot about your religious background. From people's everyday attire, I can tell you who is a Christian, a Muslim, or a Jew. I can even tell you which sect they belong to. For example, Arab Christians often wear a large cross on a chain around their necks to show they are Christians and proud of it. Some even have a cross tattooed on their arm or back.

Jesus was stripped completely of His clothing—those outward signs of a man's identity, his place in society that makes him someone. Jesus's public stripping meant He was no longer anything at all. He was reduced to an outcast, despised by everyone.

Jesus's stripping reminds us of Adam and Eve's expulsion from the garden of Eden. God's splendor fell away from humans, who now stood naked and exposed, unclad and ashamed. On Calvary, Jesus took on the condition of fallen man. Stripped of His garments, He reminds us that we have all lost the first garment of God's glory.

Nothing is mere coincidence. Everything that happened to Jesus is contained in God's divine plan and revealed in His Word. The Lord passed through all the stages of man's fall from grace. For our sake, the Sinless One even became sin (2 Cor. 5:21). But each step He took, for all its bitterness, became a step toward our redemption.

Lots were drawn for Jesus's cloak, "woven from the top in one piece" (John 19:23). This can also be taken as a reference to the high priest's robe, which was "woven from a single thread," without stitching.[7] Jesus, the Crucified One, is our true High Priest.

## *Jesus's Remarkable Intentionality*

In crucifying Jesus, the Roman soldiers were only doing what had been prophesied about Him long ago. Psalm 22, for instance, written by King David one thousand years before Jesus was crucified, depicts a man crying out to God for deliverance in the face of horrible persecution. The psalm contains unmistakable parallels to the New Testament account of Jesus's crucifixion—the piercing of His hands and feet with nails (v. 16), the parting out of His clothing (v. 18), and more.

It was what Jesus chose to happen and, in many ways, caused to happen. He had preached that God alone was the true King whose kingdom was at hand, challenging the political-military rule of Rome. He worked miracles and gave profound spiritual teachings, rivaling the authority of the Jewish leaders and priests. In the eyes of both Roman and Jewish officials, Jesus posed a threat.

Then He rode into Jerusalem on a donkey like a messianic king as the crowds cast palm branches before Him. A donkey is a symbol of humility and poverty, whereas riding a horse is a symbol of victory and power, but there's no question that the palm branches gave a strong message. To the crowds, they symbolized freedom from the Roman occupation. Of course, Jesus was there to accomplish much more than political liberation; He wanted to free the people from sin. But the Romans didn't see it that way. And in Jerusalem, His overturning the merchants' tables in the temple court didn't endear Him to the Jewish leaders.

Jesus was no passive victim. He knew in advance that Judas was planning to betray Him and even urged Judas to do so (John 13:21–27). He did not defend Himself before the Sanhedrin or before Pilate. Jesus did not call down legions of angels to deliver Him, as He could have done (Matt. 26:53). When He was led out to be crucified, He took up His cross and carried it to Golgotha because He had chosen the path of suffering. He knew it was the will of God. Only in this way could He fulfill His messianic destiny and the prophet Isaiah's vision of the Suffering Servant of God, the one who was "despised and rejected by men, a Man of sorrows and acquainted with grief" (Isa. 53:3). As that Servant, Jesus

> [bore] our griefs
> And carried our sorrows; . . .
> But He was wounded for our transgressions,
> He was bruised for our iniquities;
> The chastisement for our peace was upon Him,
> And by His stripes we are healed.
>
> (ISA. 53:4–5)

———

*Dear Lord, You chose to walk the way of the cross for each one of us. You were stripped of Your clothes. The soldiers humiliated You, and You felt alone and naked. But they were simply doing what God had willed and You had freely chosen. Because You took up the cross, I can take up life in its fullness. Because You were led to die, I will have eternal life. Because You bore my sin, I can receive Your forgiveness. Dear Lord and Savior, let me learn to forgive others. Give me a servant's heart.*

# CHAPTER 11

# Jesus Is Nailed
# to the Cross

The actual act of crucifixion begins like this: The soldiers grab You roughly and shove You onto your knees before the crossbeam where it lies on the ground. You offer no resistance as they flip You, naked and covered with blood and grime, over onto Your back and stretch out Your arms over the wood.

STATION

XI

The soldiers are quick, brutal, and all business. Two of them kneel at either end of the beam. One holds down an arm with both hands, leaning on it hard to immobilize it against what is about to come. As for the other . . .

You feel a sharp point position itself momentarily against Your wrist below Your left hand, where the structure of the bones and tendons can support Your full weight on the cross as You writhe through the ensuing hours. The next instant, *thunk!* goes a heavy hammer, and simultaneously Your eyes and mouth open wide from the shock of instant, indescribable pain as the metal spike drives through Your muscles and severs Your nerves.

Do You scream? The Bible does not say. Tradition keeps You

silent, but You are not a tradition. You are a flesh-and-blood man, and Your body is fully alive to the agony of this moment.

*Thunk!* The other nail tears into Your right wrist, affixing it to the crossbeam. No matter how submitted You are to Your Father's will, Your body strains against the torture. But the soldiers, powerful, experienced, and unrelenting, restrain You, unwittingly assisting You in your mission.

*Thunk! Thunk!* Deeper go the nails through each wrist, securing You to the patibulum as blood wells from the wounds.

*Thunk! Thunk!* Those who have come to watch stand motionless and impassive. Through a daze of pain, You can hear a few women weeping nearby.

"Good enough. Let's hoist Him up," one of the soldiers says, and the next moment they are dragging You back up to Your knees and then to Your feet, and then they muscle the crossbeam—and You— up into position on the crucifixion pole, well above the ground. You hang there, Your arms outstretched, all Your weight dragging at the two thick, black nails that jut out below Your hands. Your feet, suspended over empty air, will not dangle there for long. Even now, strong hands grip Your ankles. . . .

## ✖ The Eleventh Station

**The eleventh station is located inside the Church of the Holy Sepulcher, just behind the wall of the tenth station. It is marked by the lavishly ornate Roman Catholic (Franciscan) altar of Calvary, also known as the Latin Calvary.**

The altar was a gift from Italy's Ferdinand I de Medici. He was made a cardinal in 1562 at the age of fourteen but was never ordained into the priesthood. If you look up, you will notice a decorated blue ceiling with an eleventh-century mosaic of Jesus in the center. The more modern mosaics above the altar illustrate the crucifixion, the women at the foot of the cross, and the binding of

Isaac. The nave leading into this side area was designed in 1937 by Antonio Barluzzi. The vault features a twelfth-century mosaic of Jesus being nailed to the cross.

### Where Was the Real Golgotha?

The gospels of Matthew, Mark, and John say that the place of crucifixion was called Golgotha, which is a Greek transliteration of the Aramaic word *gûlgaltâ*, meaning "skull." English translations of Luke's gospel call the location Calvary, from the Latin *calvariae locum*, which means "place of the skull."

From early times, Christian tradition has identified Golgotha as the place we're presently standing, under the large dome of the Church of the Holy Sepulcher. Yet since the first century, scholars have debated whether this site was outside the walls of the city, as Scripture implies. Many believe it was and that archeology supports their conclusion. However, since the nineteenth century, others have believed Golgotha was in present-day East Jerusalem on a rocky outcrop known as Gordon's Calvary, north of Damascus Gate and very near the Garden Tomb and the East Jerusalem bus station. Gordon's Calvary does look a bit like a skull, but Golgotha may have gotten its name not from a rock formation but from the fact that so many people were crucified there.

The precise location of Golgotha is not clear in Scripture. John 19:41 says there was a garden in the place where He was crucified. Moreover, Hebrews 13:12 records that Jesus "suffered outside the gate." Under Jewish law, the remains of the burnt offering—a bull, a sheep, or a goat—had to be taken outside the city gate and burned, and the ashes were dumped there as well (Lev. 4:8–12). Of one thing we can be certain: Jesus Himself was such a complete sacrifice.

##  The Curse That Became Our Blessing

In the ancient world, the Assyrians were the most notorious for practicing crucifixion. In the Israel Museum, a replica of a relief from the palace of Sennacherib shows Jews impaled on poles outside the conquered city of Lachish in 701 BC. Sometimes people were hung up on the outside of a city wall; at other times they were pinned to trees or impaled. The bodies were left for scavengers such as vultures, hyenas, and wolves. They were probably not buried.

In contrast, while Jewish law allowed a man to be put to death for a capital offense and his body hung on a tree, it stated, "His body shall not remain overnight on the tree, but you shall surely bury him that day, so that you do not defile the land which the LORD your God is giving you as an inheritance; for he who is hanged is accursed of God" (Deut. 21:23). In Jesus's case, Jewish law also required His burial before the Sabbath started. The Scriptures say He died at about the ninth hour of the day (nine hours after sunrise), or approximately 3:00 p.m., so there was little time left to entomb Him.

In other words, Jesus experienced the most accursed death of His culture. The high priests made sure of it by referring Him to Pontius Pilate. A Jewish court would have sentenced Jesus to death by stoning, which did not carry a curse, but that wouldn't satisfy the Jewish leaders' lust for vengeance. The cursed death of crucifixion would also put an end to any messianic speculation—or so they hoped.

But the mode of Jesus's death, far from undermining His messiahship, fulfilled it. On the cross, Jesus became the curse that removed our curse. As the apostle Paul wrote in Galatians 3:13, "Christ has redeemed us from the curse of the law, having become a curse for us (for it is written, 'Cursed is everyone who hangs on a tree')."

Crucifixion did not, could not, snuff the movement Jesus started. That is because an event followed that no one had in their wildest dreams anticipated.

The resurrection.

Suddenly Jesus's crucifixion appeared in a glorious new, redemptive light. The resurrection explains why, in the temple courtyard, Peter and John preached Christ crucified. Their message was a paradox: they believed He was the Messiah, yet He was cursed. To quote Paul again, "We preach Christ crucified, to the Jews a stumbling block and to the Greeks foolishness" (1 Cor. 1:23). The whole notion of a Servant Messiah was ridiculous to the secular, Hellenized world.

That is hard to grasp in modern culture, where the cross is an accepted and honored religious symbol and the stuff of many a Christian song. Not so in antiquity; then the cross was what it really was: an appalling, accursed death.

> Then one of the criminals who were hanged blasphemed Him, saying, "If You are the Christ, save Yourself and us." But the other, answering, rebuked him, saying, "Do you not even fear God, seeing you are under the same condemnation? And we indeed justly, for we receive the due reward of our deeds; but this Man has done nothing wrong." Then he said to Jesus, "Lord, remember me when You come into Your kingdom." And Jesus said to him, "Assuredly, I say to you, today you will be with Me in Paradise." (LUKE 23:39–43)

Three men being crucified in torment. One taunts Jesus, demanding a salvation he thinks Jesus can't deliver. The other, sensing something different about Jesus and perhaps aware of the events of His trial, defends Him as innocent.

To this second man, Jesus makes an astonishing promise: "Today you will be with Me in Paradise."

*Today?* Jesus had been on the cross only an hour or two, and most crucifixions lasted several days before the victim finally died from exhaustion, exposure, loss of blood, and suffocation.

And *Paradise?* The word comes from a Persian word meaning "walled enclosure," and later, "garden." It described a place of beauty, harmony, and joy—in Jewish thought, the lost garden of Eden: a high, holy place in the presence of God. It was a world away from the mount of crucifixion.

Jesus's promise to the thief puzzles Christians who believe salvation comes only by confessing Jesus verbally as Savior and Lord. It's unlikely that this man prayed the "sinner's prayer." Somehow he simply recognized who Jesus was and, in his hour of terrible need, cried out to Him. Jesus saw his heart and responded.

God is "rich in mercy" (Eph. 2:4). He saves us not because we have earned salvation or deserve it but because He is merciful.

## 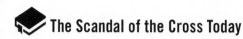 The Scandal of the Cross Today

As I write, Iraqi Christians are being crucified by ISIS, or ISIL, the Islamic State of Iraq or the Levant. Hundreds of Christians have been crucified and thousands killed in the name of religion. In June 2014, one man survived crucifixion in Syria after the jihadists raided his village near the Turkish border and nailed him to a cross for eight hours as a punishment. Eight other men from Deir Hafer village in Aleppo province died from the same punishment. They were crucified "in the main square of the village, where their bodies will remain for three days."[8]

The Islamic State (IS) first emerged during Syria's civil war in the late spring of 2013. It was initially welcomed by some Syrian rebels, who believed the combat experience of IS soldiers would help to topple President Bashar Assad. But their subsequent horrific acts of brutality quickly turned the Syrian opposition, including some Islamists, against ISIS. Rebel forces launched a major anti-ISIS offensive in January 2014 and pushed them out of large swaths of Aleppo province and the northwest. However, ISIS remains firmly entrenched in Raqa, its headquarters in northern Syria, and it wields significant power in Deir Ezzor in the east near the Iraq border.

In response to ISIS's atrocities, the Christians in my neighborhood formed a parade in June 2015, walking through the Christian quarter and declaring our faith, that we are not afraid of persecution. We are willing to die for our faith, and no one can take the cross from us.

The symbol of the cross is not welcome in Israeli society and is very offensive to some, mostly because of the Holocaust and the tragic history of European Christians persecuting the Jews over the centuries in the name of the cross. Once, as I was guiding a group from South Africa down the Via Dolorosa, a dozen Orthodox Jews came down the nearby steps while we were praying at the sixth station, and three of them suddenly spat on the cross our group was carrying. Remembering how the Roman soldiers had spat on Jesus (Matt. 26:67), I saw the Bible come alive in the middle of the Via Dolorosa. I explained to my group that these men were from a small sect of exceedingly religious Jews who dislike hearing about Jesus or passing by a church or a cross, and such incidents happen from time to time with these people.

No person, no time, and no place is too cursed for God not still to be there. The great psalmist-king David wrote, "If I make my bed in hell, behold, You are there" (Ps. 139:8). For the disciples, preaching Christ crucified meant they believed Jesus had achieved something profound through a death that had made Him a curse. He had overcome death and hell. No one can say, "I have gone too far for God to help me."

---

*Dear Jesus, I cannot bear to think of the pain You suffered being nailed on the cross so that I could be set free. Many of Your followers in the Middle East are partaking of Your suffering today. Help them, and help all of us who love You, wherever we are, not to return pain to others in return for the pain they inflict on us. Above all, help us put all our faith and hope in You. Help us focus on the cross no matter what happens. Increase our faith, I pray. Help us to tell others that You are there for them, no matter what their situation and suffering may be. I pray for justice and for the light to prevail over the darkness in this part of the world.*

# CHAPTER 12

# Jesus Dies
# on the Cross

Three hundred sixty torturous minutes-by-minute have crawled by since the Roman soldiers hoisted Jesus, His wrists transfixed to the patibulum, onto the crucifixion post and then nailed His feet to the wood. More hammer blows. More torn flesh. More blood. More pain.

STATION

XII

That was just after nine o'clock in the morning. On Pilate's order, one of the soldiers tacked up a wooden sign to the top of the pole above Jesus's head. In Aramaic, Hebrew, and Greek, it says, "Jesus of Nazareth, the King of the Jews" (John 19:19).

The Jewish elders protested to Pilate. "Change it to 'He said, "I am the King of the Jews,"'" they requested. But Pilate refused (vv. 20–22).

Jesus's mother, Mary Magdalene, and Mary the wife of Clopas, accompanied by the disciple John, have moved close to the cross to keep watch over the sacrificial Passover Lamb they know as teacher, friend, and beloved son.

 **The Twelfth Station**

The twelfth station is located at a Greek Orthodox altar inside the Church of the Holy Sepulcher. Under the altar, a silver disk with a central hole is said to mark the spot where the cross stood, and pilgrims kneel and reach inside the hole to touch the top of Golgotha. The lines here are usually long. My advice: come early, around 6:30–7:30 a.m., when the lines are much shorter.

It was right about noon when gray clouds began to move in from the west and cover the sun. Luke tells us that "there was darkness over all the earth until the ninth hour" (Luke 23:44). The darkness is more than cloud shadow; it is elemental, such that even "the sun was darkened," as if by an eclipse (v. 45). An eerie silence reigns over Calvary, draped like a blanket over the landscape. Only the labored breathing of the dying men can be heard. They are slowly suffocating, and their senses are growing numb.

> Now there stood by the cross of Jesus His mother, and His mother's sister, Mary the wife of Clopas, and Mary Magdalene. When Jesus therefore saw His mother, and the disciple whom He loved standing by, He said to His mother, "Woman, behold your son!" Then He said to the disciple, "Behold your mother!" And from that hour that disciple took her to his own home.
>
> (JOHN 19:25–27)

Except for "the disciple whom [Jesus] loved," traditionally believed to be John, all the men who followed Jesus have deserted Him. But some faithful women remain to the end. All four gospels mention them,[9] and John's gospel says that Mary, the mother of Jesus, is among them. Now, as He feels the darkness closing in on Him, Jesus entrusts His mother to the care of one of His dearest friends and followers, a man whom He knows will faithfully carry out His request.

Why not one of Jesus's siblings? The Bible doesn't say. We know little about the other children of Joseph and Mary. Jesus's younger half-brother James later became one of the main leaders of the believers in Jerusalem, but that is further on, and Mary knows nothing of what will be. All she knows is the bitter, bitter present. She is swallowed up in anguish, watching her firstborn son die.

Since her visitation by the angel Gabriel more than thirty years ago, Mary has known that Jesus's destiny would be unique. At the child's dedication in the temple, the ancient Simeon had spoken disquieting words to Mary: "This Child is destined for the fall and rising of many in Israel, and for a sign which will be spoken against." His old eyes peering into hers with both intensity and compassion, he warned Mary: A sword would pierce her own heart as well (Luke 2:34–35).

Moreover, events throughout her Son's life were marked by His own cryptic sayings. Jerusalem at age twelve: "Did you not know I had to be about my Father's business?" A wedding feast gone wineless at about age thirty: "My hour has not yet come." Jesus's words, like signposts, have pointed through the years to a strange, difficult life for Mary's Son, stamped with sorrow for a mother's heart. Mary always knew that she too would know grief. But nothing has prepared her for this sword that now, true to Simeon's words, pierces her soul at last.

"I am thirsty," Jesus cries. A soldier comes forward and proffers, on the end of a reed, a hyssop sponge soaked in wine mixed with myrrh. Giving a crucifixion victim sour wine or gall to dull his senses was common practice. But Jesus refuses. His cup is unmingled pain, and He will drink it to the last (John 19:28; Mark 15:23).

"I am poured out like water," Psalm 22 says prophetically,

> And all My bones are out of joint;
> My heart is like wax;
> It has melted within Me.
>
> My strength is dried up like a potsherd,
> And My tongue clings to My jaws;
> You have brought Me to the dust of death.
>
> (PS. 22:14–15)

Jesus cries out again, agony in His voice: *"Eli, Eli, lama sabachthani?"* His words, echoing the psalm's first verse, mean, "My God, my God, why have you forsaken me?" (Matt. 27:46).

One more time, drawing on a last reserve of strength, Jesus calls out loudly:

> Father, into your hands
> I commit my spirit.
> It is finished.[10]

They are His final words.
His head drops. His last breath whispers from His lungs.
Jesus is dead.

■  ■  ■

> At that moment the curtain of the temple [which safeguarded the holy of holies] was torn in two from top to bottom. The earth shook, the rocks split.　　(MATT. 27:51 NIV)

Suddenly the whole landscape lurches into motion. It rocks. It grinds. Clouds of dust billow as the heaving ground ruptures. There on the reeling hilltop, where the body of Jesus hangs between heaven and earth in the darkness, even the seasoned soldiers shake in their military boots.

> When the centurion and those with him who were guarding Jesus saw the earthquake and all that had happened, they were terrified, and exclaimed, "Surely he was the Son of God!"
> (V. 54 NIV; CF. MARK 15:39)

Luke 23:47 gives the centurion's words a different nuance: "Certainly this was a righteous Man." "Righteous" is a literal translation of the Greek word *dikaios*. It is a remarkable declaration about Jesus by a centurion hardened by long experience crucifying rebels and criminals who were anything but *dikaios*. From the start he has sensed, from Jesus's attitude and words even in the midst of His acute suffering, that something about this condemned man was very different. Now he is sure. The man was innocent of any wrongdoing. He was righteous. And nature itself is venting its anger at the monstrous injustice.

##  From Separation to Wholeness

They were some of the hardest words I've ever heard: "Andre, I'm leaving my position as managing partner of Twins Tours & Travel. I need to be a tour guide only."

I was stunned. Tony, no longer my partner? My brother and I did everything together. Twins Tours was *ours*. How could I manage it without him?

I felt like a dead man—and when I got beyond the initial shock, I cried like a baby. To me this was the end of Twins Tours. For weeks my heart ached. A huge part of me was identified with my brother and what we did together; now it was like half of my being had been severed from me. I felt so broken.

Yet it was at the climax of my brokenness that I came to better appreciate the immensity of Jesus's sacrifice on our behalf. For in the midst of losing my twin and closest friend as my managing partner, I remembered that Jesus too had experienced the hardest separation of all. Dying on the cross, He was separated from His heavenly Father.

It is in life's painful passages that we discover our true self. Sometimes we can't know who we really are because we are in our own way. God will bring circumstances to remove our pride and shallow self-identity so our eyes become focused on Jesus and His vision for us. Jesus is the only source of healing. Let His light shine on and through you as you discover your place in Christ. As you heal and grow stronger, those around you will be transformed as well.

There is incredible power in discovering who God really means you to be. The joy and happiness are indescribable. Life's journey is still full of struggles, but when you surrender to God, you find true purpose. Jesus surrendered His life and brought salvation to mankind. It was worth all the pain. So too, when you find who God intends you to be, you will feel that everything you've suffered was worth it.

I went to many people seeking advice about the business, and all of them told me not to shut down the office but to keep the tours going. I did, and what I considered the worst event in my life became a great blessing to me. I not only survived, I thrived. The suffering stage was important in order for both my destiny and my brother's to be released completely and finally.

Today Tony focuses on guiding and using his skills fully, and he helps in the office when he is not guiding. Stepping down as managing partner with me was the best decision he could have made for both of us. The separation allowed each of us to discover our individual identities, for although we are twins, we have different callings in life.

 ## Getting Our Priorities Straight

Separation and pain can, in time, be healing and the pathway to our true identity and calling in life. Suffering is necessary if we are ever to grasp the implications of who we are in Christ.

This teaching clashes with the prosperity gospel that has dominated the thinking of many in the West, who claim that following Christ should bring health and wealth. In that "gospel," there is no place for suffering. But that is just not reality, and such thinking will only generate more confusion around the world—particularly in those areas where Christians are persecuted for their faith.

The world seeks to get what it wants by any means—stealing, suing, cheating, killing, even religious duplicity. This is not what Christianity is all about. Becoming a millionaire or a president or a ruler is not the greatest thing you can do with your life. No, the greatest thing you can do is die for your faith. This is real Christianity, and understanding this is where we learn to die to the flesh and live in the Spirit. The West is asleep to this reality and to what is happening around the world to their brothers and sisters in Christ.

Early Sunday morning on October 7, 2007, the body of twenty-six-year-old Rami Ayyad was found near The Teacher's Bookshop in Gaza City. The recipient of regular death threats for managing the city's only Christian bookstore, operated by the Palestinian Bible Society, Rami was kidnapped the previous afternoon at 4:30 as he closed up the shop.

He was still alive at six o'clock Saturday evening, when he phoned his wife to let her know he'd been abducted and would be returning home later that night. But sometime in the next few hours, his abductors shot and stabbed him to death. Then they dumped his body off by the store, leaving his two young children fatherless and his pregnant wife a widow.

Rami was a vibrant Christian who helped lead Gaza Baptist Church's Awana club and directed the church's summer children's camp. His death was the latest and cruelest act of violence directed against Christians, and against the bookstore in particular, by militants who wanted it closed. They had already bombed it twice. Then came Rami's murder.

As one who lives in a part of the world and in the Middle East where many, like Rami, could die for our faith, I must tell you that physical death is not the worst thing that can happen to you. The loss of integrity, the loss of Christian values—the loss of your soul—are worse than enduring a cheating pastor, divorce, or mockery for your faith. If I must be martyred for my faith, then so be it. Christians are being killed all over the world, and persecution is on the rise. What is happening all over the Middle East will one day reach the United States. You can count on it. The Western church needs to be ready.

This may require preachers to stop whitewashing reality and start telling it like it is—to stop tickling the ears of their parishioners and start awakening Christians to the world we live in. We need more mature Christians who know the truth and are united in the face of it—before it is too late.

■   ■   ■

Persecution and martyrdom are part of the pattern of identifying our lives with the life of Jesus, the Suffering Servant of Isaiah 53:

> He is despised and rejected by men,
> A Man of sorrows and acquainted with grief.

And we hid, as it were, *our* faces from Him;
He was despised, and we did not esteem Him.

Surely He has borne our griefs
And carried our sorrows;
Yet we esteemed Him stricken,
Smitten by God, and afflicted.
But He was wounded for our transgressions,
He was bruised for our iniquities;
The chastisement for our peace was upon Him,
And by His stripes we are healed. . . .

By His knowledge My righteous Servant shall justify many,
For He shall bear their iniquities.
Therefore I will divide Him a portion with the great,
And He shall divide the spoil with the strong,
Because He poured out His soul unto death,
And He was numbered with the transgressors,
And He bore the sin of many,
And made intercession for the transgressors.

(ISA. 53:3–5, 11–12)

Because Jesus was wholly righteous, He was able to make many others righteous: "For He made him who knew no sin to be sin for us, that we might become the righteousness of God in Him" (2 Cor. 5:21). Jesus took our place in suffering the death penalty that our sin requires. He was able to do this because He was the Righteous One. In exchange, we receive His righteousness and are brought back into relationship with the living God.

———

*Dear Lord, thank You for being the Righteous One. Thank You for Your perfect life and Your sacrificial death on the cross. Help me to embrace the reality of the cross in my own life as part of that transaction, whether in small sacrifices or persecution and even martyrdom for Your name's sake. You never promised us an easy life—You promised us an abundant one. Help me to allow*

*You to determine what "abundant" looks like in my own life. And thank You for taking my sin upon Yourself and giving me Your righteousness in exchange. Like the centurion, I look upon Your cross today with wonder. Thank You for loving me like that!*

# CHAPTER 13

# Jesus Is Taken Down from the Cross

When a person dies in the Old City in Jerusalem, hundreds of friends and neighbors visit the family to comfort them in their loss. But at the end of the day, the family is left alone. So it was in Jesus's day as well, and so it is with His death in particular. The crowds have scattered; only Mary, John, and Jesus's immediate family remain— except for two others who have been watching from afar.

STATION

XIII

Nicodemus and Joseph of Arimathea, a respected member of the Jewish ruling council, are well aware that time is growing short. In scant hours the sun will set and the Sabbath will begin. Now Joseph, who opposed the council's actions, approaches Mary with his request: "May I honor Jesus by burying Him in my own new tomb? It has never been used."

It is a great kindness. In those days, the bodies of crucifixion victims were often left to rot or be consumed by scavengers. Joseph, desiring that Jesus be properly buried so that His bones can later be interred in an ossuary, offers his own property as the final resting place. The tomb would be safely sealed by a heavy stone rolled across the entrance. Will Mary agree?

Yes, says Mary, numbly. Thank you.

Meanwhile a soldier, checking on the crucified men, is surprised to see that Jesus is already dead. To make sure, he drives his spear into Jesus's left side, piercing his heart. The torso sways from the thrust, but not a muscle twitches, and out of the wound comes a mix of blood and water—a sure sign that the crucified man has expired.

The two other victims are still alive and struggling for breath, but "the Jews did not want the bodies left on the crosses during the Sabbath and they asked Pilate to have the legs broken and the bodies taken down" (John 19:31 NIV). Breaking the men's legs removes the support they need to inhale, thus ensuring rapid suffocation. The agonized breathing ceases.

Joseph hands the soldiers Pilate's written instructions giving him charge over Jesus's body. "He's all yours," the soldiers say to him and Nicodemus. "Take Him down whenever you're ready."

## ✘ The Thirteen Station

**Like the last three stations, the thirteenth station is also located in the Church of the Holy Sepulcher. It is located just inside the main entrance, where you will see a slab of stone around which people are kneeling and praying. This is the Stone of Anointing or Unction Stone.**

According to tradition, the body of Jesus was laid on this slab after being removed from the cross. The belief is rooted in first-century Jewish custom. Bodies of the dead were usually prepared for burial on a large stone a few hours after the person had passed away. They were anointed with spices and wrapped with linen strips. The procedure was generally done by family members, so it was a very personal ritual.

The Anointing Stone commemorates the faithfulness of Nicodemus and Joseph of Arimathea, who prepared Jesus's body for burial. This is a highly venerated Greek Orthodox site, but the lamps hanging over the stone were donated by Armenians, Copts, Greeks, and Latins. Tradition aside, it is not the stone on which Jesus's body was prepared for burial; this one is from the eleventh-century Crusader era and was placed in this location in 1810. At that time the church underwent complete reconstruction in order to keep it from crumbling from extensive fire damage sustained in 1808.

## ♡ Insights for Your Heart

Nicodemus and Joseph carefully lower Jesus's body and, according to tradition, place Him in the arms of His mother. There Jesus rests, as He did so often when He was a babe. At His birth, He was the weakest king in the world. Now in death He is once again powerless, cradled tenderly in the arms of His mother, Mary of the sword-pierced heart.

This is how our Lord loved us. He emptied Himself for us who abandoned Him. It is our sin that caused His death. Every soul except His deserves Calvary; every sin of ours is a nail in His cross. He wants us to hold Him, as Mary held Him, close to our heart.

The sun is lowering toward the horizon. There is little time left to inter Jesus before the Sabbath begins. Nicodemus lays a gentle hand on Mary's shoulder. "We must take Him," he says. Mary looks up at him with red, tear-filled eyes and nods. She does not want to let go, but she knows that she must.

Nicodemus has brought a hundred pounds of myrrh and aloes. "Then [the two men] took the body of Jesus, and bound it in strips of linen with the spices, as the custom of the Jews is to bury" (John 19:40).

Having finished their work, Nicodemus and Joseph wrap the body in a white linen cloth and carry it to the tomb.

##  Tribute to My Father

When my twin and I were around seven years old, my father, Yousef Antone Moubarak, would sit in his favorite chair and, holding one of us in each arm, tell us stories from the Old Testament. Not so much from the New Testament—I don't know why; perhaps he thought we could learn it easily by ourselves when we grew up. In any case, the Old Testament stories were his specialty, and with his vivid imagination and knowledge of the Scriptures, he set us inside the ancient dramas enacted in the land we lived in.

Dad was a well-educated man who read and wrote fluently in Arabic, Italian, French, English, and Hebrew, and who also spoke some Spanish and German. He invested his intellect and inventiveness in those priceless Bible story times with his sons. Tony and I listened, enrapt, as he told us how David vanquished the giant Goliath in the Elah valley just a twenty-minute drive from our house. He told us many other stories as well about King David and his son Solomon. Dad also captivated us with tales of the Sinai desert, where Moses wandered with the Hebrew people for forty years after God saved them from captivity in Egypt. We could picture the mighty walls of water looming on either side as the Hebrews passed through the Red Sea to freedom on the far shore.

Dad told us how, at the end of the Hebrews' desert wandering, God at long last guided them into the Promised Land. On our father's lap we listened to the story of Joshua and the battle of Jericho. We imagined Joshua's army marching around the city and the walls crashing down as the rams' horns sounded.

From the book of Psalms, our dad showed us the goodness of God and the emotions of the human heart, and from the Song of Songs he taught us about Jesus's love for His church. Dad would tell us of all these things and more while my brother and I played with his goatee and his hair until we became sleepy. Then our big, strong father would carry us both to bed.

■  ■  ■

My father was a policeman in the Israeli police force. Many times he got phone calls in the middle of the night. Then he would put on his uniform, take his gun, and go out on a job. Often he came home after midnight or even in the early morning. It was hard, tiring work, and many days we missed having our dad at dinner with us. Mom would explain that he was at work and would come home late. Then we would feel sad because we would miss his great stories. But mostly we missed him.

On days when Dad was home for dinner, afterward he often would lie down on his bed and take off his shoes but not his uniform, because he was so tired. My mother would lie next to him and listen as he expressed his frustration with his hard job, doing her best to comfort him as he tried to relax.

One day he came home about six o'clock in the evening. He was so exhausted that he put his gun on the table in the living room instead of in the special locked cupboard in his bedroom. After dinner he laid down on his bed while my twin and I played cops and robbers in the living room. I was the thief and Tony was the policeman. Tony grabbed the gun, fully loaded, off the table and pointed it at my face.

From his bed, my father saw us. In the blink of an eye, he jumped from his bed, ran over, and snatched the gun from Tony. A couple of seconds later and I might not have survived to write this book. I'd never seen my father so upset and serious. He grounded us in our room for the next twenty-four hours.

### The Day I Lost My Father

My father served in the Israeli police force for fifteen years. His job put our family in a difficult position as Christian Arabs living in Jerusalem. However, my dad was highly respected by all our neighbors and friends and in the community. He was known as a just man of strength and honor. His name, Joseph, means "Provider" in both Aramaic and Hebrew, and that is what my father wanted to do: provide fair treatment, security, and decent conditions not just for his family but for his community. He wanted to make a difference in the dark side of Jerusalem and work for justice to make our city a better place to live.

Wherever I went around the city, I was proud to be the son of Mr. Joseph Moubarak. When I applied for my first job at the American Colony Hotel, they asked how I was connected to Mr. Joseph Moubarak. I replied with a huge smile that he was my father, and as soon as they heard that, I was accepted for the job. After a couple of years, I moved to Christ Church's Heritage Center Museum, located opposite the Central Police Station inside Jaffa Gate, where my dad served as a policeman.

About 12:30 one quiet day at the museum, while taking my half-hour break, something inside me told me to go home quickly. It was the Holy Spirit. I had been working a long time at the Heritage Center and had never left work during a break. But that day I decided half an hour was enough time to go home, have lunch with my parents, and return to work.

When I arrived, my father was sitting in his favorite chair where he used to tell us his stories. His eyes were closed. Dad liked to nap in that chair every afternoon, and I did not want to wake him up. Since my mother was not home, I prepared some of my favorite food, sat beside my father, and started to eat. Five minutes passed. Suddenly my dad made a strange noise and his eyes flipped open. I knew immediately that he'd had a stroke or a heart attack.

I screamed, "My dad is dying!"

The time was 12:45. I ran to the phone, dialed 101 for the ambulance, and was told they would be there in fifteen minutes. Then, dashing back to the living room, I laid my father on the floor, raised his legs onto the couch, and started to do CPR—once, twice, three times, but there was no response. The third time, I tried mouth-to-mouth resuscitation. By the fourth time, I was panicking because I could see I was losing him. I heard one of his ribs break under my hands from pushing on his chest.

Suddenly my dad gave a long sigh, and I knew at that moment that I had lost him. My father was dead.

"My dad! My dad!" I screamed. All my sadness and hurt went into those words. My mother and some of the neighbors heard me and came running, my mother screaming and wailing hysterically.

The phone rang. It was the ambulance saying they were not allowed to enter to the Old City by themselves because it was not safe; they had to wait for an Israeli security escort. They were at New Gate, only seven minutes from my house, but when I offered to escort them, they said it wasn't permitted. I screamed into the phone that my father was dying and they had to come *now*. Then I hung up and returned to my father.

My dad was lying in the middle of the living room. I began to cry like a child.

The medics arrived a couple of minutes later at 1:30 with three escorting soldiers. "Where have you been?" I shouted in Hebrew. "It took you a long time to come, and now it is too late. Why? Why? Why?"

They checked my dad, put something on his mouth, and gave him an injection to try to save his life. But I knew even before the medics came that I had lost my father right in my own hands. My best friend. It was the end for me. Already I missed talking to him and playing with him. My father was so young, only fifty-seven years old. I felt that the devil had taken his life early, and I was mad at the devil.

■ ■ ■

My father's funeral was held the next day in the Maronite Church near Jaffa Gate. The church was packed, and even the small court-yard outside the church was full of people. The bigger courtyard up the steps was also packed, and the crowd spilled out into the street outside the entrance gates to the church.

I heard later that on the morning of his death, Dad had helped an old lady all the way up the big, steep steps from the market to the Christian quarter. On the last day of his life, he was helping someone in need. That is why my father was so universally revered and why almost the whole community came to honor him. And it is one of the many reasons why I myself loved and respected my father as a boy, cherished him as his grown son, and will always love and miss him: Yousef Moubarak—my friend, my role model, my hero, my dad.

## ♡ The Great Cure

After my father's funeral, his four sons—Tony, Albert, Alfred, and I—carried the coffin from the church to the main street at Jaffa Gate, all the way to Zion Gate, through the parking lot, and down the hill opposite the Hinnom Valley to the cemetery. As I laid my father in the tomb, I thought of how Jesus's body, like my father's, was placed in a tomb, and that thought gave me comfort.

Life in this world is a series of joys and sorrows, of hopes that come to life but also of dreams that die, of deaths small and great, until ultimately each of us faces that last and greatest death. It is the one certainty in this life, the final affliction for which there is no cure.

Except One.

Jesus, in His mortal body, put death itself to death and buried it in His tomb, then rose from the dead to secure eternal life for all who believe in Him. Only the Son of God could do that. He is our great and shining promise. Only what goes into a tomb can be resurrected.

> But now Christ is risen from the dead, and has become the firstfruits of those who have fallen asleep. For since by man came death, by Man also came the resurrection of the dead. For as in Adam all die, even so in Christ all shall be made alive. . . . When this corruptible has put on incorruption, and this mortal has put on immortality, then shall be brought to pass the saying that is written: "Death is swallowed up in victory."
>
> > "O Death, where is your sting?
> > O Hades, where is your victory?"
> >
> > (1 COR. 15:20–22, 54–55)

---

*Dear Jesus, You commanded us to honor our father and mother. I surely honor my father—he cared so much for his family and loved us greatly, and I miss him very much.*

*Many of us who have lost one or both of our parents feel such sadness. How we wish our dad or mom were still with us! Thank You for the great gift they were to us. We commit them to You, knowing that You love them far better than we ever could. Thank you, Jesus, that because You are the resurrection and the life for both our parents and us, one day we will see them again, forever young, in the joy of Your eternal brightness.*

# CHAPTER 14

# Jesus Is Laid in the Tomb

*Joseph took the body, wrapped it in a clean linen cloth,*
*and placed it in his own new tomb that he had cut out*
*of the rock. He rolled a big stone in front of the entrance*
*to the tomb and went away. Mary Magdalene and*
*the other Mary were sitting there opposite the tomb.*

MATTHEW 27:59–61

STATION

**XIV**

A s the trumpets of the temple priests echo across the
city, welcoming the beginning of the Passover Sabbath,
the Lord of creation is laid to rest in the Earth He created. And so
the cycle of Jesus's human life has run its course. His stepfather,
Joseph, found an earthy stable for His birthplace; another Joseph
has provided a rock tomb for His burial. Jesus was wrapped in soft
cloth as a newborn; now in His death, once again He is swaddled
in white.

But there is one last parallel that goes back much further, back
to a garden in the Eden of a newborn world. There the Lord God
put the first Adam to sleep, and from his side God took a rib and
formed it into Adam's bride, Eve. Today on the cross, as the Last
Adam hung in the sleep of death, His side was likewise laid open,
and from it, symbolically, will come forth His bride, the church.

 **The Fourteenth Station**

Above the Anointing Stone is a mosaic on the inner wall depicting Jesus's burial. To the right are a crucifixion image and steps that descend here from the site where Jesus was crucified. To the left lies the tomb, the fourteenth—and last—station of the cross. Head that way and enter the rotunda of the Holy Sepulcher beneath the larger of the church's two domes.

In the center is the Edicule, or "Little House," a small chapel built in the sixteenth century, flanked by rows of huge candles. Inside are two rooms. The first holds the Angel's Stone, allegedly a fragment of the large stone that sealed Jesus's tomb, and in the second is the Tomb of Christ—the Holy Sepulcher itself. This is the final station of the Via Dolorosa.

Because pilgrims over the centuries constantly laid their hands on the tomb, wearing down its surface, a marble plaque was placed on it in the fourteenth century to prevent further damage.

Under the Status Quo agreement of the eighteenth century, the Old City was divided into four quarters, and the existing division of responsibilities for the various sites of importance to Christians, Muslims, and Jews was preserved. The Eastern Orthodox, Roman Catholic, and Armenian Apostolic Churches were given rights to the interior of the tomb, and each of them celebrates the liturgy or Mass there every day. The site is also used for other special ceremonies, such as the Easter Saturday ceremony of the Holy Fire led by the Greek Orthodox Patriarch.

The Status Quo agreement also deemed that the tomb itself, hewn in the side of a limestone cave, was under the jurisdiction of the Greek Orthodox Church. To preserve its ancient character and its importance as a symbol of early Christianity, the Greek Orthodox Church has never renovated the tomb. However, in October 2016, scientists took advantage of a brief sixty-hour window allotted them to remove the tomb's protective marble exterior, extant since at least the mid sixteenth century and probably long before. At first nothing more than fill material was discovered. But continued work revealed an astonishing discovery: yet another marble slab with a cross inscribed in it—and finally, on October 28, the original burial bed, intact.

> "I'm absolutely amazed. My knees are shaking a little bit because I wasn't expecting this," said Fredrik Hiebert, National Geographic's archaeologist-in-residence. "We can't say 100 percent, but it appears to be visible proof that the location of the tomb has not shifted through time, something that scientists and historians have wondered for decades."

In addition, researchers confirmed the existence of the original limestone cave walls within the 19th-century Edicule, or shrine, which encloses the tomb. A window has been cut into the southern interior wall of the shrine to expose one of the cave walls. . . .

Archaeologists have identified more than a thousand such rock-cut tombs in the area around Jerusalem, says archaeologist and National Geographic grantee Jodi Magness. Each one of these family tombs consisted of one or more burial chambers with long niches cut into the sides of the rock to accommodate individual bodies.

"All of this is perfectly consistent with what we know about how wealthy Jews disposed of their dead in the time of Jesus," says Magness. "This does not, of course, prove that the event was historical. But what it does suggest is that whatever the sources were for the gospel accounts, they were familiar with this tradition and these burial customs."[11]

Once again current archaeological findings corroborate the biblical account, this time circling around the most compelling event in human history: the resurrection of Jesus Christ. The full article includes reasons why the site may in fact be what centuries of tradition have claimed it is—the actual burial site of Christ. (For more on the authenticity of the Holy Sepulcher, see appendix C.)

Of course, whether it really is Christ's tomb can never be proved or disproved. What matters is, the results help to confirm the credibility of the gospel writers who recorded Jesus's resurrection and believed in it with all their hearts—so much so that they and others like them devoted their lives to proclaiming that message. They took seriously the words of Jesus: "You shall receive power when the Holy Spirit has come upon you; and you shall be witnesses to Me in Jerusalem, and in all Judea and Samaria, and to the end of the earth" (Acts 1:8).

## ♡ A New Journey Begins

Thus ends the journey of the Via Dolorosa, the Way of Grief. That is, so it ends if you stop at the fourteenth station. But there is more. For here at this tomb, at this place of death and seeming finality, a new kind of life was birthed—resurrection life, powerful and imperishable. And here, at what to all appearances was the end of the road for Jesus and His followers, a new journey commenced: the beginnings of a faith that would change the world.

―――――

*Lord Jesus, I believe in Your resurrection power. I trust in You and I love You. May the victory of Your resurrection spread its peace from Jerusalem throughout the Middle East and all over the world. May it inspire the people living near Your "tomb of glory" to overcome prejudice and hate—for Muslims, Christians, and Jews to grow in love and respect for one another. Your death was no pretense. Because You really died, You experienced the ultimate penalty for our sin. Your very real death opened the door for me to experience real life. All I can say is, "Amazing grace! How can it be, that Thou, my God, should die for me?"*

*Jesus, I believe there is a fifteenth station. There is a life of power and sacrifice, of glory and pain and love in the Spirit. For while Your tomb is empty, my own grave has yet to be occupied, and meanwhile, eternal life is meant to be lived here and now as well as in Your coming kingdom. Please show me what that means for my life. Come alongside me, Lord, and guide me beyond the fourteenth station. Take me on a journey of discovering the power of Your resurrection, both in the lives of my brothers and sisters in far-off lands and in my own life, day by day.*

# PART 3

# Beyond the Tomb

# CHAPTER 15

# The Power of
# His Resurrection

"Unless a grain of wheat falls into the ground and dies, it remains alone," Jesus told His disciples, "but if it dies, it produces much grain" (John 12:24). The Wheat Grain fell and died as it was intended to. But that was not the end. The death of Jesus was the gateway to His resurrection and to life—real life, eternal life—for countless people across the world and the ages.

And so there is, in a sense, a fifteenth station—not of the cross, but beyond the cross and beyond the tomb. It is not a physical station that you can visit. It is not even a station, really, for there is nothing stationary about it. Rather, it is a walk—a walk of relationship with Jesus, living in the power of His Spirit. The fifteenth station is where we, like Paul, come to know experientially "the power of His resurrection, and the fellowship of His sufferings" (Phil. 3:10).

In this final part of the book, I will share with you some of what that has meant for me and other Christians in Jerusalem, in Israel, in the West Bank, and in the Middle East. I hope that as you read, you will hear my heart and the heart of Jesus Himself for His church. I hope you will feel a new solidarity with us, your brothers and sisters here in this land of struggle and persecution, and that you will desire to come alongside us in practical, personal ways—for we need you, and truly, you need us. Finally, I hope you will feel challenged and inspired to deepen your understanding of what it means to live your life fully committed to Jesus and His church.

## Hagar Ministries

There was no reason for Hamal[12] to think this afternoon should be different from any other. Residing with his family in a small town near Nablus in the heart of the West Bank, he had returned home from work and was reading the Qur'an. It was a longstanding habit of his as a devout Muslim who attended the mosque every Friday.

Today, however, Hamal was tired. It was hard to stay awake as he read. His eyes grew heavy, heavier . . . he was asleep.

The next thing he was aware of was a light entering the room—a brilliant light coming from . . . where? The light seemed to have no source other than itself. But Hamal felt no fear—because powerful though the light was, it was also gentle.

The pages of the Qur'an flipped, and the light disappeared.

Immediately Hamal woke up and reached for his Qur'an. From the verses on the page, the name *Issa*—Arabic for Jesus—leaped out at him. (Muslims call Jesus *Nabi Issa*, which means the "Prophet Jesus," because they believe in Him as a prophet but not as the Messiah.)

Hamal had never heard of Christians, for no Arab Christians lived in his village. Not until after Jesus introduced Himself to Hamal through the above experience, sparking in him an unquenchable thirst to learn more about this Issa of whom his Qur'an spoke, did Hamal eventually learn of and contact Hagar Ministries. In reply, they mailed him a copy of the *Injil* (Arabic for the New Testament), and Hamal devoured it. It was wonderful! Issa was all over its pages, and He was amazing. Most marvelous of all was His love for people—including Hamal.

Now my friend and I, both of us with the ministry, had made the hour's drive from Jerusalem to Hamal's town. Parking outside a building that looked like solid concrete, we ascended a perilous staircase to the family's third-floor living quarters—about five by five yards in size, with few furnishings other than several mattresses lying randomly by the walls. We were offered the usual tea in old glass cups, soiled and stained a rusty color. In the Middle East, it is rude to refuse food or drink, so we took some sips. The tea was delicious.

"Where have you been?" Hamal said. "For so many years I've wanted to meet a Christian, talk to him, and share the experiences I had. Please do not leave!"

My heart was broken and tears came to my eyes. We Christians are so spoiled. Countless people in the world need to hear about the love of Christ, yet all too often we Christians do not care to be a testimony of the life of Christ to our neighbors still trapped in darkness.

Hamal had sent the rest of his family to work in the field, including his father and mother, so he could be alone with us. Going to a cupboard, one of the family's few pieces of furniture, he opened the top drawer and picked up the only item inside—his precious *Injil*. Hamal had read it three times since he received it. He had already learned so much from his *Injil*. He said it was the only good thing in his life. The way he treasured it moved me deeply. So many Christians own multiple copies of the Bible; few of us revere the Bible as this young man did his single copy of the New Testament. When we left, we gave Hamal all the materials, booklets, and resources we had with us.

■　■　■

Hagar Ministries was founded in 1998 by three indigenous Christians who recognized the need for discipleship among Muslim-background believers in Israel and the West Bank. The organization seeks to disciple those who are unable to be part of a local church. Hagar Ministries guides and encourages them so they will become salt and light to their families and communities. They are taught and counseled through both cell groups and personal discipleship, and many of these disciples are now powerfully mentoring others and expanding Jesus's name in West Bank villages. Both spiritually and practically, Hagar Ministries has been the gateway for other Christian ministries to also work among Muslims in the West Bank, continuing the work that Hagar ministries started.

My work with Hagar Ministries was never boring! It shaped my personality and took me deeper in my spiritual life. For three years, from 1999 to 2001, I prayed every day on my knees. My ministry partners and I would pray in the morning, invite the Holy Spirit to guide us, cover ourselves with the blood of Jesus, and then make our contacts with Muslims who needed fellowship and discipleship in West Bank villages. Every day we drove to towns like Tulkarem, Ramallah, Jenin, and Nablus. And, as in the story I just shared, God used us in remarkable ways.

One day my ministry partner and I made the two-hour drive from Jerusalem to the Palestinian village of Jenin. We had a phone number, and the person who answered gave us directions to meet him. We drove until we reached a wide-open valley of expansive fields, known as the Dothan Valley in the Bible. Its rich soil produces the best vegetables in all the West Bank. The Dothan Valley is where Joseph was first imprisoned in a well by his jealous older brothers as they decided his fate, then sold as a slave to a passing caravan and taken to Egypt. Joseph's brothers covered their sin by lying to their father and saying that a wild beast had killed his favorite son.

I think I might have felt a bit like Joseph. Here we were, in the middle of nowhere; if something happened to us, no one would know about it. It was very scary. But we were filled with the Holy Spirit and continued to pray for God's protection.

A young man appeared and stared at us for about thirty seconds. Then he came over and hugged my friend and me. "Finally! I get to meet Christians!" he said, tears streaming down his cheeks. "Where have you been? We need you guys so much!" I saw the love of Christ in his eyes; he was full of that love.

Abdul was raised in a religious Muslim family and was taught from childhood that Jews and Christians were infidels who do not love Muslims. Therefore he should not love them, he was told. He grew up with this hatred all his life, never knowing that *Issa*—Jesus—was a loving person who loved *him*.

Then one day, bored at work, Abdul turned on the radio in his office, and on came a Christian station. Should he listen to it or not? Out of curiosity, he kept the station on—and for the first time heard a message about the love of Christ.

"When the message finished, I was in shock," Abdul said. "My parents had lied to me and told me that Christians and Jews are bad people and hate Muslims. And I had believed this big lie. Can you believe that my own parents lied to me!

"This was something big in my life, so I decided to start to search for the truth. I have turned on this channel every day for the last four years, and finally I got connected with you."

Abdul gave us another hug and said, "Thank you for the loving hearts you have. I lacked this love all my life. I did not understand the meaning of love before. I had no feeling, but *Issa* restored my life, and I am alive and can love other people."

This man had never seen a Christian before in his life and had certainly never hugged one. We sat with him for half a day, gave him another Bible, and did a Bible study with him about how Jesus left everything, including His throne, and came down to earth because He loved us.

*Brothers and sisters, just show the love of God in your heart and life. Many people will notice that you are different and will come and ask you about it. They too need this love in their life. Show a loving heart to the Muslims, the Jews, and any human being. This love can melt hearts of stone and make them more loving to others. The great commandment the Lord gave us was to love one another as He loves us.*                          (JOHN 13:34–35)

## Squaring Off with Demons

My work with Hagar Ministries set me up for frequent clashes with the enemy. Fortunately, I was not unprepared. Long before my involvement with the ministry, I had already experienced the reality of demons and our authority over them in Jesus's name. One of my earliest encounters happened during a revival in 1990 in the heart of the Christian Quarter.

In one of the small homes in the dark Old City, my friends and I experienced a powerful outpouring of the Holy Spirit. We gathered every Wednesday evening at 6:00 p.m., leaving the door open as an invitation to one and all. In the Christian Quarter, the houses are packed together along the narrow streets; families and neighbors live side by side and on top of each other. So when my friends and I started with worship and prayers, people would flood into the meeting. By seven o'clock the room would be full. Passersby felt drawn to come in. Some said our worship melted their hearts, and they wanted to hear more. Others even claimed they saw angels surrounding the area, and they were attracted by the sound of our prayers.

As one of the brothers shared the Word of God with us, more people would come in. The body of Christ is tiny in Israel, especially Jerusalem, and sixty people praying is a megachurch by Western standards. We always had at least that many, and sometimes up to 120 people, mostly young adults who were tired of their lives—tired of living in sin, tired of using drugs and getting drunk every day because they had no jobs. They were gifted men and women with a lot of energy but few or no opportunities to succeed in life.

The presence of the Holy Spirit at our gatherings was so strong that we were not aware of time. As we worshiped the Lord with joy, His presence would intensify. Many people were healed physically and released from demons. The revival was overwhelming and new to us, but every week, God's Spirit would lead us, and His presence would stay in the room even after we left.

One day, as three of my friends and I were walking through the Christian Quarter, a guy leaped out at us. He was half drunk, crying and cursing himself. "Help me!" he howled. "My life is destroyed!" It was a cry of despair from the bottom of his heart, and we felt compassion for him. Taking him to the prayer room, we sat him down in a chair and began to pray.

Immediately evil spirits started to manifest, and the man's behavior became very weird. I was scared to death, my knees began to shake, and I wanted to run home. *Oh Lord, what are we to do?* I thought. *We are new to this!* But the presence of the Holy Spirit was strong, and as we prayed, the Lord directed us.

An angel of the Lord appeared. We did not see him, but the demons in the man shouted, "Take this angel away! He has a huge sword of fire and he is torturing me!" The angel helped us; whenever a demon lied, the angel struck it a blow. We saw this with our own eyes. It was so real.

There were seven demons in the man, and by the power of the Holy Spirit, we released him from them one at a time. Each time, the man's facial features would change according to the nature of the demon. The last three demons were the strongest, but because of the power of the blood of Jesus, they could not stand even hearing the Scriptures when we read from the Psalms. "This is all lies, lies!" the man would shout, putting his hands over his ears. Once a demon looked through the man's eyes into mine and said, "Andre, you especially, do not talk to me."

"Shut up in Jesus's name," I commanded under the anointing of the Spirit. "I will be the one who releases my friend from you demons."

*How did the demon know my name?* I was shocked, to say nothing of scared, but the Lord gave me power. We needed to know the name of each demon because all of them were so sneaky, and they lied to us. After we got to recognize them, we understood that each one was responsible for a particular area. One demon controlled alcoholism; another, sexuality; and so on.

When demons manifest, the person usually is not aware of what is taking place. Our battle on behalf of this man finished at 3:00 a.m., and when he woke up, he asked what had happened. He knew he had been released. He was a completely different person, much more relaxed and peaceful. The man rolled up his sleeve and said he'd had a large scar on his right hand, but now it was healed! He accepted the Lord Jesus into his life and became one of the believers who attended the revival meetings.

I went home so happy and excited that I could not sleep for two days. What had happened seemed like a dream, but I had seen it with my own eyes. It was exactly like the Bible stories. Jesus gave us the authority to cast out demons—but it was still freakishly scary.

The following week my friends and I faced a similar situation, and from then on, helping demon-possessed people became our part-time job in the evening after work. We would meet in the Christian Quarter and just walk around. People came to us for help, and the Holy Spirit delivered them in the same way. I was no longer scared. Casting out demons became a normal part of our ministry. Whenever there was a need in Jerusalem, people called us, and we visited families in different villages in the West Bank area.

After I joined Hagar Ministries, my confrontations with demons continued. I can't count how many of them my teammates and I had to contend with. Once we visited a Muslim family in the West Bank village of Tobas. The conversation was normal until we mentioned the name of Jesus. Then the mother sitting on the couch started to freak out and make strange noises, the daughter knocked hard on the door whenever we mentioned His name, and the small kid who was playing in the room stared at us in a scary way. Being in that house was like a nightmare! In the spirit, we felt it would be unwise to attempt an exorcism in this house without spiritual backup. In fact, we were terrified. We ended the visit quickly, got into the car, and drove back to Jerusalem.

■ ■ ■

I'll preface one unforgettable encounter with the enemy by sharing a little background information. During the three years I was with Hagar Ministries, my teammates and I built up hundreds and hundreds of followers of Jesus Christ, all from different backgrounds. For our safety as well as theirs, we used fictitious names. I went by pseudonyms such as Lukas, or John, or Abed Elmaseeh (which means "Servant of Christ"), but never by my real name.

Because I am a Christian Arab, speak the language, and have a blue Jerusalem identity card, I can drive all over the West Bank, unlike Israeli Jews. One day two other ministry friends and I went to Ramallah, the seat of the Palestinian Authority, to meet a contact. It was not a good day for us; we had prayed hard in the office and suffered many spiritual attacks that drained us. Something was in the atmosphere—something wrong. We pressed on in prayer, but still something was going on in the spirit that we could not understand.

After driving forty minutes, we called the man, but he began to make excuses for not meeting us. Such things happened sometimes; we would drive for hours, and then the people would not show up or answer their phones, and occasionally they would misdirect us. We made the best of such situations by spending the day in prayer in whatever village we ended up at.

On this occasion, the man agreed to meet us in a parking lot during his lunch break. At the appointed time, we saw him approaching, carrying a black stick and wearing sunglasses. He was completely blind—but we did not realize it right away because he came directly to the car as if he could see us. We opened the door and he sat in the back seat beside me. My two friends up front and I immediately sensed that something was wrong with him.

"How are you, Mr. Andre?" he asked.

He knew my real name! *How?*

I was stunned. I had never met the man before, nor had I ever used my true name in communicating with him. Since then, in my many encounters with people under the influence of demons, the person (or rather, the demon) has often inexplicably known my name. This was a strong tip-off! Immediately I knew the man was demon possessed, and it was the demons talking, not the man.

My friends and I began to talk with the man about Jesus, sharing the gospel with him, but it was as if he didn't hear us. It was a strange and uncomfortable situation. The demons had displaced the man's mind. They were strong—but they could not bear the Holy Spirit inside us, and suddenly, without any explanation, the man opened the car door, got out, and continued on his way as if nothing had happened.

But something *had* happened—something really weird! My ministry partners and I also exited the car and watched the man walk off. It had been a tense experience, and we needed to unwind from it. So we grabbed lunch in Ramallah (the hummus there is really good!).

Afterward, we dropped off one of my ministry partners, and my remaining friend and I continued on toward Jerusalem. It was then that we sensed something wrong in the car. We should have prayed immediately, but we didn't, and the feeling got stronger and stronger. Finally, as we neared the Scottish Hospice in Jerusalem, we began praying—and instantly saw a demon inside the car, about the size of a football, ricocheting from one window to the other. We knew it had been left in the car by the blind man. It could not bear our prayers. We parked the car and rebuked it, and as soon as we opened a window, it went away.

The battle lasted only about three minutes from when we started praying; then we felt normal again and were full of the joy of the Lord. My friend dropped me at Jaffa Gate, and I went to have dinner with my family, then headed to Christ Church for my night shift.

■ ■ ■

There was never a dull day during my three years with Hagar Ministries. I became a very strong Christian. But after we began receiving serious death threats in 2001, I decided to quit the ministry and move on to a different stage in my life.

## Christ Church: The Heritage Center Museum

I spent the next two years studying to be a tour guide while continuing to work in Christ Church. In 2002, I was promoted to work in the Heritage Center, a small museum inside the Christ Church compound at Jaffa Gate, visited by many secular and religious Israeli Jews.

The Christ Church and the Heritage Center are run by the Christian Mission to the Jews (CMJ). It was hard for me, as a Christian Palestinian, to work for this institution, mostly because it is considered a Zionist organization in our Palestinian communities, including the Christian Quarter. I claimed I did not care what my neighbors said or thought, but that was not entirely true. Regardless, it was not a Zionist organization, and I was welcomed there and treated like family. They tried their best to be balanced and show equality.

My presence as a Palestinian Christian in this organization was so important for them. It opened their eyes to the reality of the Palestinian Christians, and my twin brother Tony and I were good examples for them. They learned a lot about the Palestinian communities from our ten years with them.

As a tour guide in the museum, I met many interesting people, mostly Jews, so I was exposed to the Jewish people as never before. They in turn were shocked to learn they were being guided by a Palestinian Christian. It was hard for them to fathom a Palestinian working in a pro-Jewish organization! "How did this come about?" they would ask—and their curiosity became a door for me to share my faith and teach that we should love everyone. Jesus came not only for the gentiles but for the Jews as well. Most of the time people would listen, and I had many opportunities to pray with Jewish men and women and plant a seed in their lives.

What an irony! God moved me from ministering to Muslims to ministering to Jewish people!

Once while I was praying inside the museum during the slow hours, an ultra-Orthodox Jew on the steps of the museum demanded, in a harsh voice, to know what the place was. I answered in Hebrew that it was a museum, and I took him to see a model of Jerusalem from the Second Temple period. This interested him, because the temple is the holiest place for the Jewish people. I discovered the importance of how I approached religious Jews; they are very smart, so I used history in order to preach the gospel.

I shared with the man what I had learned about the Second Temple period from my history classes as a tour guide. I continued with the history lessons until I arrived at Yeshua, the Hebrew name for Jesus. When he heard that name, the man opened his eyes wide. Religious Jewish people don't like to hear of Jesus. But this man was caught off guard by the fact that I, an Arab, talked so lovingly and boldly of my Jewish rabbi, Yeshua. He wanted to hear more. Taking the opportunity, I told him how Jesus had changed my heart. Instead of hating Jewish people, now I loved them—for God had created them just as He had created me, and He loves us all. In fact, He loves us so much that He gave His beloved Son, Yeshua, a Jew, to save me, a Palestinian, and all people, Jews and gentiles alike.

The man saw that I was genuine—that I had real love in my heart for Jews and Muslims and wanted them both to know about God. He had entered the museum in a tense state, so I invited him for a cup of coffee and shared with him the complete message of Jesus Christ. I could see his eyes becoming soft. He said he could not stay long but would visit from time to time to hear more. Christ Church's unique location enabled him to slip inside without anyone seeing him; his excuse, should anyone inquire, was that he wanted to use the free toilets.

We met again the following week. He was highly educated and knew the Old Testament well. Certain things in it now made sense to him, he said, and his life had changed—because, he told me, the Messiah, Yeshua, had appeared to him and he had accepted him in his heart! Now everything he had learned as a Jew made complete sense to him.

## When God Heals

In the years since I became a Christian, I have seen hundreds of healing miracles. Many occur among our tour groups as Marie, Tony, and I guide them through the land of Israel. I could tell you lots of stories. Instead, though, let me share with you the following letter as an example of a healing that took place in a group from the United States.[13]

> *In March of 2014, my daughter, Callie, was hit in the back of the head by a basketball while playing at school. Several days later*

*she was hit in the head again by a volleyball at practice. She
began having headaches that were debilitating and affecting her
vision, ability to complete schoolwork, and to sleep. She went to a
specialist in concussion recovery who advised us to withdraw her
from school until she was symptom free.*

*Week after week we continued to see her doctor, who told
us that she wasn't recovering as he had hoped she would. Callie
stayed at home day after day and week after week battling
headaches that lasted all day and all night. She doesn't remember
a time that she didn't hurt.*

*Our family had always wanted to go to Israel to see the land
where we have read and studied about all of our lives. Callie's
doctor advised us not to go because Callie's concussion symptoms
had not improved. They said that a long trip like that would most
likely make the symptoms worse and could potentially prolong
her recovery. We prayed about whether to continue with our
plans to tour Israel and felt led to go anyway.*

*We arrived after a long flight on Saturday and began our tour
on Sunday, June 29, 2014. Callie had a terrible headache that
morning and didn't feel well. It didn't help that the temperature
was in the nineties and heat is another trigger for Callie's
headaches.*

*We began our tour in Capernaum overlooking the Sea of
Galilee. Our tour guide taught on the Beatitudes. After he was
finished, we sat in a small cave overlooking the sea. He asked if
anyone had anything that they wanted Jesus to heal. Callie, who
was 12 years old, said that she wanted Jesus to heal her head
because she had had headaches for almost 4 months.*

*Andre, our tour guide, told Callie to place her hands on
the area of her head where she was hurting. He asked her if she
believed that Jesus could heal her and she replied yes. As Andre
began to ask Jesus to heal her head of the pain that she had been
experiencing, a cool, refreshing wind began to circulate in that
cave. My husband and I began to cry because we knew we were
in the Presence of the Lord.*

*Although we didn't see a visible change after Andre prayed for her, that was the last day Callie had a headache due to a concussion. We knew that we had just witnessed the miracle of healing.*

■ ■ ■

The point of these accounts is this: The same Jesus who healed the sick, cast out demons, and brought hope and joy to countless struggling hearts as he showed them the Father's love for them in word and deed, is still at work today by His Spirit through His body, the church. We are His hands, His feet, His voice. You and I are His ambassadors who proclaim His peace and love to those held captive by this world's darkness—or we can be if we will seek Him. His resurrection is real, and so are the life, the power, the vision, and the love that flow from it—from the Living One in us, and we in Him.

# CHAPTER 16

# Victory Over Death

It began with a mystery:

*When the Sabbath was past, Mary Magdalene, Mary the mother of James, and Salome bought spices, that they might come and anoint Him. Very early in the morning, on the first day of the week, they came to the tomb when the sun had risen. And they said among themselves, "Who will roll away the stone from the door of the tomb for us?" But when they looked up, they saw that the stone had been rolled away—for it was very large.*

(MARK 16:1–4)

The job had been done for them. But when and by whom? And . . . where was the body of Jesus?

The answer came swiftly, incredible and joyous beyond imagining.

*Suddenly Jesus met them. "Greetings," he said. They came to him, clasped his feet and worshiped him. Then Jesus said to them, "Do not be afraid. Go and tell my brothers to go to Galilee; there they will see me."* (MATT. 28:9–10 NIV)

The impossible had happened. Death had been put to death.

Life was given new definition—and, through its risen Author, it became the new destiny and final decree for all who love Him.

Who could refrain from sharing such astoundingly good news? It bubbled forth naturally and irrepressibly from those first wonder-struck eyewitnesses with life-giving force. And so it does still today, here in the darkest places of Jerusalem, the Middle East, and throughout the world.

■  ■  ■

Yet though many small but bright fires of faith are burning in Jerusalem, the city as a whole desperately needs a revelation of Jesus's resurrection and the power of eternal life. The Christian Quarter is Christian largely in name only. Many here are bound by addictions, violence, poverty, and hopelessness, and this is true throughout Israel. There is no hope unless the Holy Spirit brings life to its "dead bones," as described in Ezekiel 37:1–14. There, the prophet is borne by the Spirit of the Lord to a vast valley full of utterly desiccated bones.

"Son of man, can these bones live?" the Lord asks Ezekiel.

"Only You know," Ezekiel replies.

> Again He said to me, "Prophesy to these bones, and say to them, 'O dry bones, hear the word of the LORD! Thus says the Lord GOD to these bones: "Surely I will cause breath to enter into you, and you shall live. I will put sinews on you and bring flesh upon you, cover you with skin and put breath in you; and you shall live. Then you shall know that I am the LORD."'"
>
> (VV. 4–6)

The prophet speaks as commanded, and with a tremendous rattling, the bones come together and are covered with flesh and skin. Another prophecy follows, breath returns to the lifeless bodies, and a great army rises to its feet. "I will put My Spirit in you, and you shall live," the Lord declares to them, "and I will place you in your own land. Then you shall know that I, the Lord, have spoken it and performed it" (v. 14).

Like the dry bones of Ezekiel's vision, the Christian communities scattered throughout Jerusalem, the Holy Land, and all across the Middle East, especially Syria and Iraq, desperately need God's Spirit to bring them new life, strength, and hope. That which is dry and scattered is dead; we need the Holy Spirit to revive these bones. When that happens, then the Spirit of God can come upon us and unite us—all of us, regardless of where we are in the world. We can become one Christian body, functioning together with everyone using his or her gifts in the right place at the right time for the glory of God.

That is the vision that grips my heart for Israel, the West Bank, and Palestine. I long to see the churches united through revival, for the power of God to be manifested in Jerusalem, and for the good news to be preached under the anointing of the Holy Spirit. I yearn for miracles that free and bless the people of this land. And I desire that all who visit Israel from other countries be transformed, returning home refreshed and joyous, with a new vision of God to spread in their families, churches, and communities.

## My Prayer for Jerusalem's Christian Quarter

The chanting starts at 11:00 a.m., loud and bold, sung in Arabic. It is ancient, dating back to the Turkish occupation of Jerusalem in the sixteenth century, when Christians were not allowed to sing anywhere except inside the churches. Today, on this *Sabt Al Nour*— Holy Fire Saturday, the day before Orthodox Easter—their praises resound through the community, and they will not be silenced.

> *We are the Christians.*
> *We have been Christians for centuries*
> *And we shall be forever and ever here.*

Chanting traditional hymns at the top of their voices, the indigenous believers dance vigorously around Jesus's tomb at the Church of the Holy Sepulcher. Borne on the shoulders of celebrants, drummers beat out a tempo. And from across the world, pilgrims of all nationalities join them to celebrate the five-hundred-year-old annual tradition once again at the same time, in the same way, in the same place.

On this ancient holiday, a flame miraculously ignites on the Holy Tomb, and from it, the Patriarch of the Greek Orthodox Church lights a candle. With that candle he lights other candles, and those who hold them spread the flame to the candles of other celebrants, who in turn light still other candles until thousands of candles are burning brightly.[14]

My dream is that my neighbors in the Christian Quarter will, in a similar manner, carry the light of the gospel with them—not only on *Sabt Al Nour* but every day. I long for the power of Christ's resurrection to transform them and for the light of Jesus to shine through them every moment. I pray that their eyes will be opened, and that they will no longer live in the darkness and depression of the Via Dolorosa.

Our Lord walked through the sadness and hatred, the tough streets and terrible journey, of the fourteen stations of the cross. But in the end He conquered death and rose from the grave victorious. My dream is that my Christian community will experience His victory firsthand. I pray that . . .

the Christian Quarter will become a light to Jerusalem and even to the world;

its people will be anointed, filled with the Holy Spirit's power;

my friends and neighbors will wear crosses not just around their necks but in their hearts as well;

they will grow more and more humble, serving one another and standing together to carry the message of resurrection and victory because the blood of Jesus has cleansed them from sin and conquered evil.

I have so much hope—because I have seen this happen in my family and other families. As we live completely for God, life will come to the city of Jerusalem, and God will use us mightily for His glory.

The only solution for the hatred and misunderstandings between Palestinians and Jews is for both sides to bury their hatred and forgive one another—and this can only happen when they accept the love of Christ into their lives. Only this can bring real reconciliation. Jesus alone is the solution to the conflict. Christians should pray for the eyes of both Muslims and Jews to be opened to the love of Christ and to embrace forgiveness of sins and salvation through His blood. They need to die to their selfish ambitions and ask Christ to rise up within them.

This is true not only for those who live in Jerusalem and the Middle East but also for the whole world. It is true right where you live. And if you have experienced a deep grief or injustice, so that you are walking your own Via Dolorosa, it may be particularly true for you. Forgiving those who have injured us is costly, but not forgiving them is costlier still, both to us and to those around us.

Some wounds go so deep that only the grace of God can empower us to rise above them and forgive, from our heart, the persons who have inflicted them on us. But the love and power of Jesus make such forgiveness possible. We can love even our enemies once we grasp how deeply, passionately, and sacrificially we ourselves are loved by the Son of God, who gave Himself for us without reservation on Calvary. The purpose of the stations of the cross is to draw us into the reality, the mystery, and the mercy of the cross—so that we might experience the love of God with ever-increasing fullness and joy.

You and I do not serve a philosophy. A philosophy cannot give us life.

We do not serve moral principles. Moral principles cannot empower us to live up to their standards.

We serve a living, resurrected Jesus—the King of Kings, who gives us eternal life, grace to live righteously, hope beyond the struggle of our own bitter Via Dolorosas, and love beyond anything we can comprehend.

We are loved, you and I, wonderfully, wisely, fully, and forever.

For that reason, and that reason alone . . .

Beloved, let us love one another.

# An Appeal to the Churches of the West

ISIS began as an al-Qaida offshoot, the Islamic State of Iraq (ISI). As the Syrian civil war intensified, the group's involvement in the conflict was at first indirect, but differences over ideology and strategy soon led to bitter infighting. Renamed the Islamic State of Iraq and Syria, ISIS turned out to be too extreme and brutal for al-Qaida, leading to a public repudiation by al-Qaida chief al-Zawahiri, who called on ISIS to leave Syria and return to Iraq.

Then ISIS captured Mosul, Iraq's second largest city and the home of an ancient Christian community. ISIS now controlled territory stretching from the eastern edge of Aleppo in Syria to Falluja in western Iraq, and the northern city of Mosul. The group has shown its ruthlessness in crucifixions, beheadings, amputations, and other horrific brutalities.

Imagine—these things are happening today!

Non-Muslim minorities have four options: either flee, convert to Islam, pay a fine, or be put to death. There is no coexistence. Although Christians, Muslims, and Jews have lived together in this part of the world for centuries, the brand of Islam that now dominates through ISIS is so extreme that it represents an existential threat to Christians and Jews.

## What Has Happened to the Christians?

It is estimated that 200,000 Christians were living in the region now occupied by ISIS. Where are they now? Only a fraction of them has been accounted for. *Where are all the missing Christians?*

Nobody knows. Those who escaped report having all their belongings confiscated except their clothes. Jewelry, money, automobiles, even food and water were confiscated as they were forced to pass through Islamic State checkpoints. Many wives and daughters have been kidnapped and sold in an Islamic "slave market."

Decades ago, the world watched as the Jews and others, including Catholics, gypsies, and homosexuals, were rounded up and killed by the Nazis in the Holocaust. No one outside the European continent believed these people were being killed on an industrial scale. Yet they were. Today, Islamic State terrorists are posing with their victims, making videos, and even tweeting crude jokes about their carnage. They revel in their killing, yet the world is largely closing its eyes to it—and worse, to the probable spread of this darkness westward, to Europe and America.

The leading nations once solemnly promised not to allow another holocaust to happen. Yet episodes of ethnic cleansing and genocide have swept repeatedly through recent history from Cambodia to Rwanda, Nigeria to Sudan. Time and again the world has stood silent as whole populations and tribes have been exterminated, relocated, or forced into destitution.

Today in nearby Jordan, 600,000 registered refugees from recent wars live in camps, towns, and villages in terribly difficult conditions. Approximately 80 percent of the Syrian refugees in Jordan live in urban areas in the north of the country; the remaining 20 percent live in the Za'atari, Marjeeb al-Fahood, and Al-Azraq camps. Those in the guarded camps feel they are in prison because they cannot leave. Only UN or aid workers can enter.

The situation for the Syrian refugees is so hopeless that many want to go back to their own country and die there. They feel they have no future and are like cattle, rotting and waiting to die. Yet they too are part of the body of Christ, and Jesus conquered the grave and overcame hell and Satan for them.

Jesus did not stay in His tomb; He was resurrected in power and glory. My hope is that the Christians in those refugee camps will open their eyes and hearts so that the resurrected Jesus will be alive in them, and that they will grab onto His power in their lives despite their terrible situation. When they do, I believe miracles will take place, and we will have many amazing testimonies coming from those camps.

## A Wakeup Call to the Western Churches

For Palestinian Christians, the cross is the center of our identity. Each church or denomination has its own religious shape, but the cross still unifies us, especially in times of trouble. Brothers and sisters of the Western churches, we Middle Eastern Christians need to know that other Christians also care about us and the refugees and are standing with us.

We need the West to wake up.

What is happening to Christians in Iraq and Syria is strikingly parallel to the expulsion and migration of eight hundred thousand to one million Jews from Arab Muslim countries from 1948 onwards after the State of Israel was established by the United Nations.[15] Similarly, in 2014 an exodus began from Iraq and Syria as people fled the war zone and Islamist terror. It involved more than just Christians; the Yezidis, an ancient Kurdish ethno-religious community, also had to flee because they too were regarded as infidels. By the end of 2014, the total number of refugees had reached two million, many thousands of them Christians. ISIS stripped them of their identity papers and passports and forced them to leave with nothing. They had to walk all the way to the mountains and hide. But while the world has known, the help offered has been inadequate.

Millions are once again standing by in the face of evil. We Christians like to talk only, not act. We need influential church leaders in the West to bring this problem to the forefront and to connect with local Christian communities and charities in the Middle East.

Don't leave us isolated. Western Christians need to take the situation seriously. Don't just pray for peace—condemn and battle this evil.

And especially, find homes for the refugees.

Do not forget about us or deny us. We feel alone here in Jerusalem and Israel, and our sisters and brothers in Iraq and Syria are even more alone. Western churches need to care about us, listen, and give us more attention before it is too late. In time, I believe the Islamist terror and persecution of Christians will also come to the West. We Arab Christians have paid a price and learned the lessons of continuing to live in the Middle East. We want to share with you about the reality of the persecution that exists here.

## What You Can Do

Whether you are an individual, a group, or a church, one simple, practical way you can help is this: Build a relationship with us.

All it takes is you. One person can make a huge difference—and we can make a difference for you. Make an effort to connect with us. Today's technology makes it possible. We will connect you with ministries and churches in the Middle East, especially in Israel, the West Bank, and Palestine.

In general, the churches in the West are tremendously blessed and yet so spoiled. They talk, talk, talk, but when it comes to action, they excuse themselves. We indigenous Christians are doing the hard work and still standing, persevering, and carrying our cross daily, even if it costs us our lives.

We are your link to reach the Middle East.

Please do not forget us or ignore us.

We invite you to come visit this land. You will be as safe as if you were walking the sidewalks of your hometown—perhaps even safer—as thousands of visitors from the West will tell you, and you will be in the best of hands. Let us share with you in person our narrative and heritage and help you discover the land in which our common faith is still rooted.

■ ■ ■

Jesus died and was resurrected to give us hope. Life for us Palestinian Christians often becomes very difficult here when there is open conflict, and many times I have thought of closing the Twins Tours office and moving away from Jerusalem permanently. However, I continue to hold on and hope for better days to come. I am always optimistic and looking for what Christ is doing even in the dark hours. I stay faithful and committed despite the obstacles constantly being thrown at us.

My heart and aim is that Christians in the West will become more aware of what is happening with their brothers and sisters in the East. I hope this book will inspire you to reach out to us, your Middle Eastern families in Christ. And I hope you will respond to our invitation to experience the living faith of Jesus Christ here in the Holy Land.

# Who Are the
# Maronite Christians?

I belong to a little-known denomination called the Maronites. The Maronite Church dates back to early Christianity. It is one of the few Christian denominations in which ethnicity, heritage, and faith remain vitally connected, giving it a unique spiritual identity. We still pray in the ancient Aramaic language that Jesus and His disciples spoke every day and everywhere except in the synagogues, where the Scriptures (*Tanach*) were read and prayers said in Hebrew.[16]

As the disciples of Jesus began to spread the new faith of Christianity, the Syro-Phoenicians in the coastal area of southern Syria were among the first to be converted. They were Aramaic speaking, like Jesus and His disciples, but used a Syrian dialect. Among them was St. Maron, a fourth-century monk and ascetic who dwelt in the Syrian mountains. Maron's personality was characterized by a deep serenity, an ascetic lifestyle, and constant prayer, and his mystical charisma attracted many followers. After his death in AD 410, his followers built a monastery in his memory and founded a Christian movement that became known as the Maronites. Maron's rich spirituality and his austere way of life have colored Maronite culture until the present day.

The Maronite movement reached Lebanon when St. Maron's first disciple, Abraham of Cyrrhus, the "Apostle of Lebanon," set out to convert the people through his master's teachings. The Maronites have had a profound influence in Lebanon ever since, and in spite of adversity, their community has continued to prosper for centuries. In later persecutions, they retreated to the mountains of Lebanon, creating a safe haven that absorbed other Christians fleeing over the centuries, especially during the Arab Muslim invasions of the mid-seventh century.

In the fifth and sixth centuries, the Byzantine rulers tried to impose a patriarch on the Maronites, but the Maronites insisted on staying autonomous. With the rise of Islam, Byzantine leaders recognized the strategic advantage of the Maronites in Lebanon and Syria and supplied them with weapons in the hope that they would push back the Muslim invaders. But the Maronites were distracted by their own struggle to remain independent, and the internal divisions in the Byzantine empire helped to facilitate the Muslim conquest of Eastern Christian territories by end of the seventh century.

Under Islamic rule, the ethnically Syro-Phoenecian Maronites began to speak Arabic, although their dialect retained Syriac peculiarities, and Aramaic is still spoken in a couple of rural villages. The Maronites were allowed to remain Christian, but they were allotted the inferior Dhimmi status and required to wear black robes and black turbans for easy identification. They were also forbidden to ride horses.

As a result of the four-hundred-year blockade between the Islamic and Roman Catholic empires, the Maronites were effectively isolated from Western Christendom. They were forgotten until the Crusaders stumbled across their community in the late eleventh century on their way to Jerusalem and established political and military alliances with their long-lost spiritual brothers. A few Maronites accompanied the Crusaders and settled in Jaffa. The Church in Rome was unaware that the Maronite Church still existed, but the Pope was quick to reestablish relations.

Today the Maronite Church is an Eastern Catholic church, in full communion with the Holy See of Rome and accountable to the Pope. It is the only Eastern church that is entirely Catholic, with no Orthodox counterpart. It is also the most Latinized and Western influenced, although Syriac, a form of Aramaic, remains the liturgical language. The Mass is conducted in Arabic, but certain short prayers during the Mass and some hymns are still in Syriac Aramaic.

Maronites served as the first tour guides of the Holy Land for visiting Europeans—first the Crusaders, then pilgrims. In the sixteenth century, the Franciscans sent priests to establish schools, clinics, and other charitable institutions, and Maronite families helped the Franciscan priests establish their mission centers. Most Catholics in the Israel and Palestine area were originally Maronite families serving the Franciscans, and they were eventually assimilated to become Latins or Roman Catholics. The Maronites benefited from higher education and were prominent in the cultural renaissance of the Middle East in the late nineteenth century.

In the twelfth century, the Maronite community came under the protection of France, and the French language and culture was widely diffused among them. Numerous French interventions over the centuries, with some assistance from Rome and European powers, helped to keep Maronite communities relatively safe but could not always protect the Maronites from aggressive neighbors like the Druze. In the massacre of 1860, 360 villages, 560 churches, and 50 monasteries were destroyed, and 20,000 people were killed. This caused a new exodus which scattered the Maronites around the world. During the First World War, an estimated one third of the Maronites died or were exiled. After the collapse of the Ottoman Empire in 1917, Lebanon and Syria came under the French Mandate, primarily because of France's long relationship with the Maronites.

Although reduced in numbers, Maronites remain one of the principal ethno-religious groups in Lebanon, and they continue to represent a majority of Lebanese people when the Lebanese diaspora is included. The present head of the Maronite Church, Patriarch Mar Nasrallah Boutros Sfeir, is the Maronite Patriarch of Antioch and all the East. He lives in Bkerke, north of Beirut, and has about seven million in his flock, 800,000 of them in Lebanon and more than six million scattered across the globe.

Israel has about ten thousand Maronites, of whom 7,500 are locals—3,500 in Haifa, 1,800 in the village of Jesh in Lower Galilee, 1,000 in Nazareth, 200 in Isfiya, a Druze village near Mount Carmel, 500 in the Akko area, and 500 in Jerusalem. The remaining 2,500 are the families of the South Lebanese Army; they came to Israel as refugees after their Israeli allies withdrew their troops from Lebanon in the year 2000.

The local Maronite community has passed through many hardships. For example, during the war of 1948, they abandoned two of their villages, Mansoura and Kfar Baram, after the Israeli forces promised them that they could return in two weeks' time. The Israeli government subsequently reneged on that promise, and so until today the Maronites are waiting for it to be kept.

In Jerusalem there are only ninety families in a single parish, making the Maronites probably the smallest Christian sect in the Holy City. They have no private schools, no marching band, and no altar in the Holy Sepulcher church. They can be found in only one place—the Foyer Mar Maroun in the Old City, near Jaffa Gate.

The Foyer Mar Maroun compound includes a Maronite convent, the archbishop's residence, a guesthouse for pilgrims, a chapel with regular services, a bell from Lebanon, and the offices

of Peregrinatio Jubilaum Jerusalem, a pilgrim organiza
in 1999. The building is maintained by three nuns of th.
of St. Therese of the Child Jesus. The archbishop, Paul Say)
based in Haifa and is in charge of parishes in Israel, Jerusalem, .
Amman, Jordan.

# The Authenticity of Jesus's Passion

Christians consider at least three passages of the Old Testament to be prophecies about Jesus's death on the cross. The first and most obvious is Isaiah 52:13–53:12, written in either the sixth or eighth century BC. This prophecy describes a sinless man who will atone for the sins of his people. By his voluntary suffering, he will save sinners from the just punishment of God. Here is a well-known excerpt:

> He has no form or comeliness;
> And when we see Him,
> There is no beauty that we should desire Him.
> He is despised and rejected by men,
> A Man of sorrows and acquainted with grief.
> And we hid, as it were, our faces from Him;
> He was despised, and we did not esteem Him.
>
> Surely He has borne our griefs
> And carried our sorrows;
> Yet we esteemed Him stricken,
> Smitten by God, and afflicted.

> But He was wounded for our transgressions,
> He was bruised for our iniquities;
> The chastisement for our peace was upon Him,
> And by His stripes we are healed.
>
> (ISA.53:2–5)

The second prophecy of Christ's passion is the ancient text that Jesus Himself quoted while He was dying on the cross: *"Eli, Eli, lama sabachthani?"* ("My God, my God, why have You forsaken me?") Jesus was quoting a verse from Psalm 22, in which the writer, King David, foretold the sufferings of the Messiah. Again an excerpt:

> I am a worm, and no man;
> A reproach of men, and despised by the people.
>
> All those who see Me ridicule Me;
> They shoot out the lip, they shake the head, saying,
> "He trusted in the LORD, let Him rescue Him;
> Let Him deliver Him, since He delights in Him!" . . .
>
> Be not far from Me,
> For trouble is near;
> For there is none to help.
>
> For dogs have surrounded Me;
> The congregation of the wicked has enclosed Me.
> They pierced My hands and My feet;
>
> I can count all My bones.
> They look and stare at Me.
>
> They divide My garments among them,
> And for My clothing they cast lots.
>
> (PS. 22:6–8, 11, 16–18)

The third main prophecy of Christ's passion is from the Wisdom of Solomon, or, simply, Wisdom. Protestant Christians place this writing in the Apocrypha, while Roman Catholics and the

Eastern Orthodox Church place it among the deuterocanonical books. It was written about 150 BC, and many have understood its verses to be a direct prophecy of Jesus's passion:

> "Let us lie in wait for the righteous man, because he is inconvenient to us and opposes our actions. . . . He professes to have knowledge of God, and calls himself a child of the Lord . . . and boasts that God is his father. Let us see if his words are true, and let us test what will happen at the end of his life; for if the righteous man is God's son, he will help him, and will deliver him from the hand of his adversaries. Let us test him with insult and torture, that we may find out how gentle he is, and make trial of his forbearance. Let us condemn him to a shameful death. . . ." Thus they reasoned, but they were led astray, for their wickedness blinded them. (WISDOM 2:12–13, 16–21 RSV-CE)

In addition to the above, at least three other, less specific messianic prophecies were fulfilled in Jesus's crucifixion:

> Many are the afflictions of the righteous,
> But the LORD delivers him out of them all.
>
> He guards all his bones;
> Not one of them is broken.
>
> (PS. 34:19–20)
>
> They also gave me gall for my food,
> And for my thirst they gave me vinegar to drink.
>
> (PS. 69:21)

> "They will look on Me whom they pierced. Yes, they will mourn for Him as one mourns for his only son, and grieve for Him as one grieves for a firstborn." (ZECH. 12:10)

# The Authenticity of the Holy Sepulcher Church

Although it is not certain, there is reason to believe that the Church of the Holy Sepulcher could, as has long been claimed, be located over the actual tomb of Christ. The most important supporting evidence consists of the following:

- In the early first century AD, the site was a disused quarry outside the city walls. Tombs dated to this period had been cut into the vertical west wall left by the quarrymen.

- The topographical elements of the church's site are compatible with the gospel descriptions, which say that Jesus was crucified on a rock that looked like a skull outside the city (John 19:17), and that there was a grave nearby (John 19:41–42). Windblown earth and seeds watered by winter rains would have created the green covering on the rock that John calls a "garden."

- The Christian community of Jerusalem held worship services at the site until AD 66 (according to historians Eusebius and Socrates Scholasticus, who wrote several centuries later).

- Even when the area was brought within the city walls in AD 41–43, it was not built over by the local inhabitants.

The early Christian community of Jerusalem appears to have held liturgical celebrations at the site they regarded as Christ's tomb from soon after the resurrection until the city was conquered by the Romans in AD 66. In AD 135, Emperor Hadrian filled in the quarry to provide a level foundation for a temple to Aphrodite; the site on which Constantine's Holy Sepulcher Church was built two centuries later had such a temple to the goddess.

The Israeli scholar Dan Bahat, a former city archaeologist of Jerusalem, has said, "We may not be absolutely certain that the site of the Holy Sepulcher Church is the site of Jesus' burial, but we have no other site that can lay a claim nearly as weighty, and we really have no reason to reject the authenticity of the site."[17]

# The Praetorium

The chief difficulty in determining Jesus's path to Calvary is that nobody knows the site of Pontius Pilate's praetorium, where Jesus was condemned to death and given the crossbeam of His cross to carry through the streets.

There are three possible locations:

- **Herod the Great's Palace or Citadel**, which dominated the Upper City. The remains of the citadel complex, with its Tower of David (erected long after King David's time), are just inside the present Jaffa Gate. This is the most likely location.
- **The Antonia Fortress**, a vast military garrison built by Herod the Great north of the temple compound and with a commanding view of the temple environs. The Umariyya School, now the location of the first station of the cross, is believed to stand on part of its site.
- The **Palace of the Hasmoneans**, built before Herod's time to house the rulers of Judea. It was probably located midway between Herod's palace and the temple, in what is today the Jewish Quarter.

The trial of Jesus before the Romans, where the procurator Pontius Pilate sentenced Christ to death, is believed by some to have taken place in a part of Herod's palace. But its exact location and the route taken by Jesus to the place where He was crucified and buried continue to be hotly debated by archaeologists, historians, Christian spiritual leaders, and scholars.

*Praetorium* is a Latin term referring to the tent of a general in a Roman encampment. Some scholars reason that Pilate's praetorium would have been located in the Roman military barracks at the Antonia Fortress. However, others say Pilate would have been a personal guest of King Herod, and therefore the trial took place in the palace compound.

Archaeologists backed by the Israeli government believe they have found the site of Jesus's trial near the Tower of David Museum in Jerusalem. The building was being excavated as part of plans to expand the Tower of David Museum, and beneath it, an old prison was discovered which was in use when the area was under the control of the Ottoman Turks and the British.

While peeling back the layers of the prison, archaeologists discovered fabric-dyeing basins dating back to the Crusades, together with foundations, walls, and an underground sewage system, all possibly belonging to the huge palace built by Herod the Great. After his death, his palace became Roman property, and archeologists believe the Roman procurators of Judea who ruled after Herod used it. That includes Pontius Pilate, who every year came from Caesarea to Jerusalem during the time of the Passover to oversee security during the festival the Jews called the Feast of Jerusalem. This is why some archaeologists consider the wall of Herod's Palace here at this site to be the only known vestige of the site of Jesus's trial.

# Stations of the Cross
## Traditional and Biblical Compared

In 1991, Pope John Paul II introduced a revision of the fourteen stations of the cross, designed to align in every respect with the biblical record.[18] The chart on the next page compares the traditional and the revised, fully biblical stations.

| TRADITIONAL | BIBLICAL |
| --- | --- |
| | 1. Jesus on the Mount of Olives (Luke 22:39–46) |
| | 2. Jesus, betrayed by Judas, is arrested (Luke 22:47–48) |
| | 3. Jesus is condemned by the Sanhedrin (Luke 22:66–71) |
| | 4. Peter denies Jesus (Luke 22:54–62) |
| 1. Jesus is condemned to death | 5. Jesus is judged by Pilate (Luke 23:13–25) |
| | 6. Jesus is scourged and crowned with thorns (Luke 22:63–65; John 19:2–3) |
| 2. Jesus takes up the cross | 7. Jesus takes up the cross (Mark 15:20) |
| 3. Jesus falls the first time | |
| 4. Jesus meets His mother | |
| 5. Jesus is helped by Simon the Cyrene to carry His cross | 8. Simon of Cyrene helps Jesus to carry His cross (Luke 23:26) |
| 6. Veronica wipes the face of Jesus | |
| 7. Jesus falls the second time | |
| 8. Jesus meets the women of Jerusalem | 9. Jesus meets the women of Jerusalem (Luke 23:27–31) |
| 9. Jesus falls the third time | |
| 10. Jesus is stripped of His garments | |
| 11. Jesus is nailed to the cross | 10. Jesus is crucified (Luke 23:33, 47) |
| | 11. Jesus promises His kingdom to the good thief (Luke 23:33–34, 39–43) |
| | 12. Jesus on the cross; His mother and His disciple (John 19:25–27) |
| 12. Jesus dies on the cross | 13. Jesus dies on the cross (Luke 23:44–46) |
| 13. Jesus is taken down from the cross and given to his mother | |
| 14. Jesus is laid in the tomb | 14. Jesus is placed in the tomb (Luke 23:50–54) |

# Notes

1. The term "living stone" is used only in the Middle East. It conveys the idea that in the midst of Israel's archaeology (dead stone), its indigenous people still remain in this land of vast history. We are part of God's story—thus, "living stones."

CHAPTER 1: **Jesus Is Condemned to Death**

2. Josephus, *Antiquities*, 18.3.2.

3. Philo, *Embassy to Caligula*, 299–305.

CHAPTER 2: **Jesus Takes Up the Cross**

4. Josephus, *War*, 5.11.4.

CHAPTER 6: **Veronica Wipes the Face of Jesus**

5. For a discussion of prophecies pertaining to Jesus's passion, see appendix B.

CHAPTER 9: **Jesus Falls the Third Time**

6. Nablus is the Arabic name; in biblical Hebrew, it is Shechem.

CHAPTER 10: **Jesus Is Stripped of His Garments**

7. Josephus, a 3, 161.

CHAPTER 11: **Jesus Is Nailed to the Cross**

8. "Daily Star, Lebanon: Isis Crucifies 8 Rebels in Aleppo," *Orthodox Christian Network*, July 5, 2014, http://myocn.net/daily-star-lebanon -isis-crucifies-8-rebels-aleppo.

CHAPTER 12: **Jesus Dies on the Cross**

9. Matt. 27:55–56; Mark 15:40–41; Luke 23:49; John 19:25.

10. Luke 23:46; John 19:30.

CHAPTER 14: **Jesus Is Laid in the Tomb**

11. Kristen Romey, "Unsealing of Christ's Reputed Tomb Turns Up New Revelations," *National Geographic*, October 31, 2016, http://news .nationalgeographic.com/2016/10/jesus-christ-tomb-burial-church -holy-sepulchre.

CHAPTER 15: **The Power of His Resurrection**

12. Names used in part 3 may be fictitious to protect the individual's identity and safety.

13. From an email dated March 4, 2016. Used by permission.

CHAPTER 16: **Victory Over Death**

14. Holy Fire Saturday is a remarkable experience. To learn about it in greater detail, visit the Holy Fire website: www.holyfire.org/eng/.

EPILOGUE: **An Appeal to the Churches of the West**

15. "Jewish Exodus from Arab and Muslim Countries," Wikipedia, accessed May 1, 2016, https://en.wikipedia.org/wiki/Jewish_exodus_from_ Arab_and_Muslim_countries.

APPENDIX A: **Who Are the Maronite Christians?**

16. Aramaic is similar to Hebrew. For example, my family name in Aramaic is *Meborak* (מברך); in Hebrew it is almost the same, *Mevorakh* (מבורך); in Arabic it is *Moubarak* (مبارك). In English, all of them mean "Blessed." Jesus's disciples spoke a Galilean dialect of Aramaic. Maronites speak a Syrian dialect because the Maronite Church

originated in the countryside near Damascus before spreading to the mountains of Lebanon.

## APPENDIX C: The Authenticity of the Holy Sepulcher Church

17. Romey, "Unsealing," *National Geographic*.

## APPENDIX E: Jesus Meets His Mother

18. Pope John Paul II, "The Way of the Cross at the Colliseum with the Holy Father, Pope John II, Presiding: Good Friday, 2004," Office of Papal Liturgical Celebrations, website of The Holy See, accessed April 20, 2017, http://www.vatican.va/news_services/liturgy/2004/documents/ ns_lit_doc_20040409_via-crucis_en.html. From the 2004 edition; the 1991 edition had similar headings but different Scripture texts.

# About Twins Tours & Travel

*The Twins Tours & Travel Managers.*
*From left to right: Marie, Andre, Tony, and Albert.*

Founded by Andre and Tony Moubarak in 2006, Twins Tours & Travel specializes in creating custom tour packages to the Holy Land, allowing travelers to explore the land where Jesus once walked and experience the Bible's living history firsthand. Today it is owned and operated by Andre and his wife, Marie, with Tony focusing on teaching and guiding groups. As we retrace the paths of the patriarchs and walk in the footsteps of Jesus, it is our aim that every traveler gains greater insight into the Scriptures and a new understanding of the land where Judaism and Christianity were born.

*Andre and Marie Moubarak* have a combined total of twenty-five years in the tourism industry. Married since 2007, they blend together the East and the West in their relationship. Together they manage and operate Twins Tours & Travel, through which they strive to cultivate long-term relationships and partnerships for the kingdom of heaven.

*Andre* is a licensed tour guide, tour operator, and gifted Bible teacher. His teachings strengthen the faith of tour participants by offering new insights into Scripture, causing the stories of the Bible to come alive. An indigenous Christian from the Old City of Jerusalem, Andre is passionate about connecting visitors with both the ancient and the modern while focusing on what God is doing today throughout the Holy Land and within the local community of believers.

*Marie* is the director of program and partnership development at Twins Tours & Travel. She has a heart to see visitors and pilgrims encounter the land and the people of Israel in a meaningful way. A skilled listener, she is gifted at discerning a group's goals and vision and translating them into a customized, financially feasible tour which meets and exceeds their expectations. Initially an American tourist herself, Marie returned to Israel as a volunteer and ulti-mately married Andre.

*Tony* serves primarily as a tour guide and is also a tour operator at the office when he is not actively guiding groups. He loves to teach and help deepen the roots of people's Christian faith so they can better follow the Lord's guidance and become better disciples of Jesus. Tony says, "My goal is that your understanding of the Bible will be greatly enriched during your visit and that, through your faith and obedience to God, you will fulfill His calling."

*Albert*, working in the office, sees to the long-term and daily needs of the drivers, tour guides, and guests, arranging schedules and ensuring that such necessities as tour folders, bags, and maps are provided.

**Twins Tours & Travel's** exceptional customer retention rate is a testimony to Marie, Tony, Andre, and Albert's expertise, their commitment to excellence, their conscientious customer service, and their prayerful care for each tour participant.

> *Our TV crew had the pleasure of working with Andre Moubarak for ten days. Besides being extremely well informed on the history and archaeology of Israel and Jerusalem and superb at transferring his knowledge to others, Andre is also service minded, flexible, and polite. He was invaluable in helping us out of smaller and bigger challenges during our production period. I highly recommend Twins Tours & Travel.*
>
> Camilla Pettersen
> Production Manager, TV INTER Norway

## From Andre—A Final Word

After Tony and I started Twins Tours & Travel Ltd., we began receiving invitations from pastors and churches in many countries, especially the United States, to come and share our testimonies, teach Scripture, and present Jesus through Middle Eastern eyes.

One invitation initiated from a tour group from Living Faith Christian Center in Baton Rouge, Louisiana, led by Bishop Raymond Johnson in October 2013. I subsequently visited his church two years in a row. They visited Israel again in October 2015, and at the conclusion of their tour, Bishop Johnson ordained me as a minister of the gospel.

I travel to South Africa frequently and have conducted many healing services in both Protestant churches and Catholic charismatic churches. I have also taught and shared my testimony in revival meetings in the heart of London and other places worldwide.

God uses my wife, Marie, and me in numerous ways. Whenever we preach in churches, the presence of the Holy Spirit is strong. Healings have occurred, and many people's lives are strengthened through teaching the Word of God. Afterward, pastors have told us how their church members have changed and their churches have been revived and strengthened. We seek to carry the message of salvation and truth and to strengthen the body of Christ worldwide, encouraging people to spend time studying the Word and to be filled with the Holy Spirit.

## Our Gifts to You

People in our tour groups testify consistently to the power of their experience. Almost everyone says their life will never be the same, and many share a testimony of healing. The testimonies are so genuine and real, and they inspire me to continue.

At the end of every tour, I give each participant the URL for my YouTube channel, which contains my many videos that summarize the teachings I provide with the tours and that will, I hope, keep alive the joyful memories of their time here in the Holy Land. Now that you have completed your own tour with this book, I invite you to enjoy the same insight-filled teachings at https://www.youtube.com/user/twinstours/videos.

Also, if you are a church or ministry leader, I would like to offer you, free of charge, my 23-page Tour Organizer PDF, developed by the Twins Tours team to help you understand the tourism industry and give you guidance for organizing a group trip to Israel. See the ensuing contact information to request the Tour Organizer.

I pray that these resources will encourage you and help build your understanding of the Word of God from the Middle Eastern point of view, illuminating the Jewish roots of our Christian faith.

## *Tour the Holy Land with Us—or Invite Us to Your Church*

If you are a pastor, a church leader, or a lay person, and

- you have it on your heart to bring a group to Israel, or
- you would like us to visit your church and share insights on the land of Israel, together with eye-opening, faith-strengthening biblical teachings and preaching,

please see the contact information at the end of this section.

■　■　■

Marie and I appreciate you so much, and we will be praying for you. We believe the best for you and that you will see your dream of visiting the Holy Land come true. We would like to be part of your journey, and we will help you at every step. We would love to hear from you!

## *Contact Us*

ONLINE

E-mail: twinstours@gmail.com
Websites: http://www.twinstours.org;
www.onefridayinjerusalem.com
Follow us: http://twitter.com/twinstours
Subscribe: https://www.youtube.com/user/twinstours/videos
Circle us: https://plus.google.com/+twinstours
Facebook: https://www.facebook.com/andre.moubarak

PHONE, FAX, AND SKYPE

Telephone:

- Jerusalem office:  +972-25798159
- Mobile:  +972-545231145
- USA:  +1-512-222-3160

Fax:  +972-25798158

Skype:  twinstours

MAIL

Twins Tours & Travel Ltd.

Jaffa Rd. 97, Clal Building

Floor C2, Office #201

P.O. Box 28314

Jerusalem 91283

Israel

# THERE'S MORE!

# Twins Tours & Travel Ltd.

| HOME | ABOUT US | BRING A TOUR | MEDIA | CONTACT US | BLOG |
| --- | --- | --- | --- | --- | --- |

**Sea of Galilee**
Sailing on the Sea of Galilee

▶ 2/6

# VISIT www.twinstours.org TODAY!

CPSIA information can be obtained
at www.ICGtesting.com
Printed in the USA
LVHW112028220419
615088LV00010B/162/P